PRAISE FOR

The *Secret* to HEALING and RECOVERY

This book is an inspirational guide for anyone who has faced challenges with their health or experienced emotional trauma. Vicki encourages the reader to be in charge of their healing experience by weaving her personal struggles into a message of hope. She eloquently describes to the reader the many facets that contribute to healing with her deep understanding of the power that thoughts and feelings have on the well-being of an individual. Her insight and wisdom are only possible through someone who has experienced challenging health circumstances, for which she offers information and techniques that are necessary for the healing process.

Vicki offers a high level of compassion for her readers, and her message speaks from a place of support and wisdom. She also offers truly attainable steps which anyone can apply, no matter what kind of challenge they are experiencing.

Her caregivers guide at the end of this book holds valuable information for anyone who takes on the role of caregiver for a family member.

I highly recommend this book and greatly appreciate the wisdom contained herein.

—**Karol K. Truman**
Author of *"Feelings Buried Alive Never Die"*
& *"Healing Feelings From Your Heart"*

PRAISE (CONTINUED)

A POWERFUL resource for us today! Vicki brings wisdom and experience together so we can all see that it is time to get more involved with our well being. I love how she clearly brings the steps to our awareness so we can do something right now, today, to better ourselves for tomorrow. Care enough about yourself to read and act upon what it takes to course correct your life and feel better. Take charge of your life!

—**Kirk Duncan**
Founder of 3 Key Elements

With the resolute wisdom that comes from not only first-hand experience but also from being a loving, insightful human, Vicki holds our hand and helps us to see our challenges. She supports us with solutions as we wind our way through the experience of recovering our life from what may be a debilitating struggle. By so plainly and vulnerably sharing her story of pain and illness, she shows us the simple, actionable tools to help us recover from chronic health concerns. Vicki reminds us that it is so much more than one simple event that leads to our deepest physical challenges—and it is more than one tool, method, technique or change that is going to raise us up and out of our pain. This book is a gift of the highest order, a handbook of powerful support to help us live our best life.

—**Dr. Sarica Cernohous**
Author of *The Funky Kitchen*

The *Secret* to HEALING and RECOVERY

Copyright © 2018 by Vicki Werner

All rights reserved.

No part of this book may be reproduced or transmitted in any form or by any means, electronic or mechanical, including photocopying, recording, or by any information storage and retrieval system, without written permission from the publisher. For all inquiries please use the contact form at www.trupublishing.com.

ISBN (paperback) 978-1-941420-38-6

Cover & Interior Design: Tru Publishing
www.trupublishing.com

Editing: Robin Bethel
www.prosestudio.com

Printed in the United States

DISCLAIMER

The information contained in this book does not in any way promote or endorse any specific healing treatments or nutritional products. The author does not diagnose, treat, cure, prevent, or otherwise insinuate healing from any disease. All information in this book is for educational purposes only and is not a substitute for quality medical care. Please consult a qualified healthcare provider for diagnosis and treatment for any emotional, mental, or physical condition. Neither the author nor publisher accept any liability from the use of information contained within this book.

The *Secret* to HEALING and RECOVERY

by Vicki Werner

Tru Publishing
Boise, U.S.A

Contents

A Personal Letter to Readers ix
Acknowledgments xi
Introduction xiii
Chapter 1—The Journey 1
Chapter 2—Convalescence 13
Chapter 3—Down the Rabbit Hole 33
Chapter 4—It's All Connected 41
Chapter 5—Beliefs and Mindset 45
Chapter 6—Elements of Creation 65
Chapter 7—Nutrition 91
Chapter 8—Support Tools 105
Chapter 9—Techniques for Personal Transformation 147
Chapter 10—Protecting Your Health from Toxins 163
Chapter 11—Experiencing and Measuring Success 169
Chapter 12—Family and Caregivers Support 177
Conclusion 197
Suggested Reading 199
About the Author 200

A PERSONAL LETTER TO READERS

I may not know you personally but I recognize your craving for wholeness. What is within you also resides within me. I pray the wisdom I have received from my years of personal struggle will assist you toward healing. I pray you will continue to have hope and feel comfort in the recognition of the human spirit, as I share with you the insights and techniques that benefited me personally.

There are three universal truths that every person desires. They are to be whole, to be loved by others, and to be seen for who you truly are. Many times illness forces us to identify ourselves by the label of disease rather than our authentic self. When we identify who we are by a medical diagnosis we are asking the world to see the part of us that is wounded and feels void of wholeness, in the hope that we will be accepted by sharing our most vulnerable aspect of who we are. I sincerely hope that you will take comfort in knowing you are not alone. I pray that you will feel strength in knowing that there is within you the power to heal when you have the correct information, environment, and support tools. Within these pages I offer you that information and support. I see you as a divine creation that is whole and loved.

I also know that my way is not the only way to healing. The audacity of any individual claiming that the only way to heal is to follow the narrow view of another is disempowerment of the highest order. Your journey is yours alone. I have the greatest respect for you in retaining your choice in how you navigate illness and healing. Whether you choose an allopathic or alternative healing approach or a combination of many modalities is your God-given right. I honor every person and modality that holds intention to help in the healing process.

Fortunately, we have a greater supply of possibilities and greater access to wisdom than ever before. Many of the healing modalities available to us today were unheard of in the past. Treatment options have expanded beyond simply isolating a tumor, a disease, or an area of weakness that must be eliminated or cut out as the only option to "cure" us of the shadow within. We now often look at the body as a whole. Many healers of today view the body systemically and understand the connection and the communication between the different organs and parts of the body. There is a knowing that healing must take place on all levels in order to fully heal. I use "fully" lightly here, for once we arrive at a certain level of healing there likely will be a yearning for an even deeper level of healing.

We now know that in addition to disease reflecting physical imbalances, disease in the physical body may also be a manifestation of spiritual, mental, and/or emotional imbalances. While this knowledge is empowering, it has also brought new blame and new assumptions that warrant caution. In some circles, the language of illness has shifted from "It's not your fault that you got sick because everything is based on genetics" to "It's all your fault—you created this disease by projecting your unresolved emotions onto your own body." The guilt and shame in this belief is almost too much to bear. We need to balance the equation. Yes, we do have ownership in contributing to our health. In fact, a great deal of ownership. However, we also live in a world that uses more chemicals and toxins than ever before in history. Access to nutritionally dense foods is limited and the stress that we feel is ever increasing. It almost provides bragging rights when you can claim to live on less sleep and eat on the run, without taking stock of the long-term effects to your health. This all leads to breakdown of the body and eventually a search for healing. I hope you find your answers here.

ACKNOWLEDGMENTS

Scott, my love for you is everlasting. Thank you for your constant support and for playing full out as my husband and partner in life. You inspire me to reach beyond what is tangible and to uncover the essence of why we are truly here.

My biological children, Sharlie, Audrie, Danyen, Cloie, and Sofie, and my stepchildren, Nathan, Ricky, Kristal, Steven, and Camille. May you each hold within you the knowledge of your greatness and may you carry with you my unfailing adoration. I am here because you are here. Your presence on this planet gave me strength and purpose to heal. I love you all endlessly. Thank you for being my greatest gifts.

My dear parents James and Shariel, thank you for giving me life and for comforting me when I felt weak and afraid. You are pillars of strength and I am so grateful for your comforting arms and words of encouragement when I needed them.

Each of my siblings, you showed up in the way that I expected and needed. I love you all far deeper than language can express. Thank you for being on this planet with me. What a grand life it is to share my heart with you all.

Kirk Duncan, thank you for awakening my understanding of my purpose and for the tremendous techniques in personal transformation that you have shared with me. You reminded me of what I came to do. I appreciate your insight and your friendship and I am eternally grateful that you chose to be the messenger that you are.

The leaders in spiritual growth, healing, and personal insight, Caroline Myss, Esther Hicks and Abraham, Bruce Lipton, Gregg Braden, Joe Dispenza, Anthony William, Nick Ortner, Sharon Forrest, Karol Truman, and Deepak Chopra. You are masters in your fields and a guidepost for me and countless others. Your wisdom is sprinkled throughout this book. Thank you for expanding my awareness to the many layers of healing

Amy Kendall, Jennifer Winfield, Sarica Cernohous, Deanna Rotty, Fredericka Close, Aleksandra Dorann, and Stephanie and Kevin Mullani. Thank you for your loving prayers and holding space in my realigning. It gave me strength knowing that each of you are on my team.

Donna Stewart. I know you are still watching over me and cheering me on from the other side. I love you.

INTRODUCTION

I want to acknowledge that healing from illness is scary, isolating, and deeply personal. There are countless people currently experiencing at least one chronic illness and within each experience are multiple layers of healing and self-discovery. I have been on a mission of self-discovery for most of my adult life and consider myself a student of the wisdom of this world. When illness struck my life, I knew that I needed to learn the secrets to healing and share the wisdom with others. I sat front and center in the school of illness. Watching, learning, asking tough questions, and receiving tougher answers.

I struggled immensely, asking the void around me, "Why am I still in pain?" Each time, there was a whisper in my consciousness. "The benefits of soul growth will outweigh the struggle you are going through. You can't see it all now but trust that it will be worth it." To which I often responded, in a much louder voice, "Nothing is worth this pain and fear and misery that I am going through." As the months and years passed, my response became a little gentler and a little quieter. Maybe it really is all about growth. Maybe I chose the accelerated training in this area of my life...maybe. The reasons became less important when the wisdom I learned along the way settled into my consciousness as truth.

In my quest for healing, I experienced many healers and techniques, but ultimately, my healing was up to me. I respect bodywork, energy healing, acupuncture, and hands-on healing as treatments. However, it is my intention to provide healing techniques that can be done independently and so have not shared them as tools in this book. Every person is looking for a deeper level of personal growth and each of us must choose the route that is optimal for our own healing.

Each technique offered in this book provides insight and healing. They are simple, doable, and safe, but you are ultimately in the driver seat with complete control of your experience. Please do not limit your possibility for healing by discounting the simplicity of some of the techniques offered. It's not the level of complexity that counts but rather the continued application of the techniques in your own life. No matter what type of healing you are searching for, these techniques have the power to help you, drawing upon no more than your own dedication and commitment to heal.

I encourage you to have an open mind regarding information that may be new to you. There may be techniques discussed that you have tried before and felt didn't work for you. Try it again. Maybe the timing is more supportive for you now. Everything shared in this book has a history of phenomenal healing support.

In no way do I believe I am an expert in what you're personally experiencing. I am not a medical doctor or a scientist. I haven't contributed to case studies with multiple blood workups and I haven't spent long nights reading medical journals with terminology that I don't understand. I haven't spent days and nights in your body and mind, feeling your pains, your fears, your struggles. Yet, I have faced enormous health challenges that led me to become an expert in communicating with my own body and understanding why I have experienced what I have. I have experienced the depths of illness, wondering many times if this day was going to be my last. Other days, I reached for that glimmer of hope that maybe one day my life will be different.

My prayers were always a hope that healing would take place. I hold hope for your healing, as well.

I know what it feels like to be among the over seven billion inhabitants on this planet and to feel isolated from life. I know what it feels like to yearn for a life that is different from the one I am currently living. I also know what it feels like to be in such excruciating physical pain that you wonder if you can endure. Day after day my body felt like a complete betrayal to my soul.

I know many of you are experiencing these same things. Some of you may be doing so while also being told by doctors that nothing is wrong or that they don't know what could be wrong.

The great paradox is that more specialty clinics and medical facilities are popping up around the country yet fewer people are receiving answers to why they are ill. Autoimmune diseases are skyrocketing and many people are walking around feeling fatigued, achy, rundown, bloated, and with an overall sense that they just don't feel right. Medical tests can't keep up with the demand for the onslaught of symptoms and disease.

We, as a country, are more medicated, in greater debt, with more demands on our time than ever before. We are overwhelmed with feelings of not being enough coupled with confusion and guilt that we can't keep up. Many of us are managing to get by but don't feel well enough to add anything more to the burdens that we already carry.

Whatever you may be experiencing, my desire is to awaken a sense of possibility within you and to remind you that you can heal—whether or not you have ever received an official diagnosis from the traditional medical community. I don't have that "magic" pill that will end struggle and pain and I don't believe that those magic pills exist. We are here to have struggle, for in the struggle lies expansion and growth. But that process can be moved through with hope.

As you read, I suggest that you have an open mind and not get hung up on language or even the techniques but rather see the message of how much healing potential is held within your own body. I make reference to God but this is not a religious book in any sense. God is a representation of an energy that is greater than me and the source of all that is. It is not necessary for you to have a religious affiliation to heal.

Thank you for your dedication to moving toward a healthier life. We are all in this together.

CHAPTER 1

The Journey

I died December 16, 2012, at 6:52 p.m. There weren't any frantic nurses running around to resuscitate me or any machines beeping in the background to notify anyone that something was wrong. Not even a family member pleading their love for me and begging me to stay. Just me in my bed, alone.

Five months prior, in July of that year, my sister Angela led a spiritual tour to Peru. My husband, Scott, and I joined the tour group, along with three of my siblings and my mother. An option with the tour was to participate in a sacred ceremony by ingesting Ayahuasca, a plant medicine containing DMT. Ayahuasca, which induces an altered state of consciousness, is used during sacred healing ceremonies under the direction of a trained shaman known as an ayahuascero. The shaman prepares the brew and offers each participant a dose, then opens the way for a spiritual awakening by whistling and singing, which escort the group deeper into a trance-like state. Although it is common for the medicine to have a purging effect through vomiting and diarrhea for up to eight hours after being ingested, this cleansing effect is considered part of the purification process.

I had experienced Ayahuasca before. Angela led annual tours to Peru and Scott and I had taken a trip with her and participated in the sacred ceremony once before in 2010. During that experience two years earlier, our tour group had crossed the river and sat in a large circle on Monkey Island, located on the Amazon river near Iquitos, Peru. It was recommended that Scott and I place ourselves at opposite ends of the circle to each have our own experience and not be emotionally pulled into the needs of the other. I sat on my thin mat looking up at the millions of stars in the sky. It was a soft moonlit night and with no light pollution, the beauty was breathtaking. The night air was comfortable but we each had a warm blanket beside us for the long cool night ahead.

Our group had traveled together for the previous two weeks and had built strong friendships with one another. There was an air of nervous anticipation for the coming hours and an overall sense of gratitude to share this experience together. As the shaman walked around the circle administering the bitter drink, I gazed upon the group, feeling safe among my new friends. Both of my companions on either side of me were men that I respected. Having them beside me gave me a sense of added protection. Listening to the muted conversations around me, my ears attuned to the sound of Scott's voice, comforting me and giving me the feeling that all was well. I had never ingested recreational or sacred ceremony drugs of any kind before and here I was about to do so, listening to wild monkeys settle in for the night on an island four thousand miles away from home.

My personal goal in this sacred ceremony was to seek physical and emotional healing, to begin to love myself, and to expand my spiritual connections. For many months prior to this excursion I felt run down on energy and often experienced digestive issues, joint pain, and low energy. I hated my body, had zero sense of my own value, and believed that I had nothing to offer the world around me. Placing my hands on my stomach I began a quiet prayer. "God, please help me to learn to love my body. Please heal my body. Please help me to know that my life has purpose. Please help me to love who I am."

I've always maintained a healthy diet and exercise regimen but looking at my stomach often repulsed me. I don't remember a time in my life that I could allow anything to touch my abdomen without feeling discomfort. Any pressure against my abdomen would cause physical distress. With an often-swollen abdomen, my wardrobe consisted of yoga pants and T-shirts, and my inner dialog consisted of a tremendous amount of negative comments about myself. I didn't feel that I had any real purpose in life and didn't believe in my worth. As a stay-at-home mother, my days were spent dutifully caring for the needs of my family, and I'd been losing all sense of autonomy. I loved my family and my role as a mother and wife but it didn't fulfill my soul. There was a chasm between the person that I was and the person I longed to become. But, I was fearful of the world. I harbored the layered emotional heaviness of being angry that my life felt so burdensome and felt guilty for not being satisfied.

As the Ayahuasca effects took hold, I was increasingly aware that my inner self was much larger than my physical body—a sensation that was too much for me to understand fully. I could hear that each member of our group was experiencing some level of discomfort from the Ayahuasca. While some barely felt any nausea, others vomited extensively throughout the night. I felt quite ill, vomiting and shaking violently.

A mist had settled on the island during the night and my teeth chattered from the chill with such intensity that my friend next to me stood up and covered me with his blanket. I watched him approach me, and in my altered state he looked like a sketched pencil drawing. Closing my eyes, I somehow knew there was a part of me that wasn't quite ready for the expansion possibilities of an Ayahuasca experience. I was grateful for the added warmth from the blanket, but was frightened by my overwhelmingly altered state. My desire was to sleep it off. I surrendered to sleep in the hope that the effects would wear off before I awakened. I awoke a few hours later feeling very sick and quite fragile, a feeling that continued for the duration of our trip. I had no desire to repeat that experience and was anxious to return home. Scott, on the other hand, loved it. He had an amazing spiritual experience and left the island feeling delirious with joy.

In 2012, Angela asked Scott to join her again. Not wanting to go without me, he enlisted Angela's help in encouraging me to try it again. Angela explained that every experience is different and the first time is often the worst, convincing me that I should have a better experience the next time. In truth, I was envious that Scott had such an incredible experience in 2010 while I chose to sleep it off. I believed that I was now ready to up my game in my spiritual quest so I finally agreed to another tour to the jungle. Unfortunately, I experienced results that were just as awful as the previous time.

I arrived home from our second trip to Peru in July of 2012, feeling out of sorts and frustrated that I was still experiencing a high level of stomach pain. I had hoped that I would have experienced a level of relief in my abdomen from the healing ceremonies in Peru but the pain in my stomach only increased as time passed. I didn't believe that the Ayahuasca was the root cause of my health concerns but that I was more sensitive to the effects due to my already compromised gut.

In August my daughter Audrie moved away to attend college the same week that my brother and his family moved into our basement while he was building their new home. It was stressful to have another family move into our personal space and I desperately missed my daughter. I was aware that something still wasn't quite right with my body but assumed that the added stress was affecting me. My nervous system seemed to always be on high alert and was extra sensitive to everyday experiences that were normal to everyone else. I continued to eat well, taking supplements to assist digestion, and tried to get the rest that I needed in hopes that my body would begin to heal, but to no avail.

In November, I was assisting my younger sister, Barbara, as a doula during the delivery of her baby. We have a very close relationship and I knew she depended on me for my willingness to be fully present and for my maternal wisdom, from having gone through this experience myself multiple times. I was massaging her while she was in transition with her labor. During a sharp contraction, I was applying counter-pressure to ease her pain when I felt my life force drain from my body and collapsed to the floor. In confusion and shock, I locked eyes with Barbara as she turned to me saying, "Vicki, I need you to be strong for me." I wanted to be strong for her and somehow mustered up a hidden source of energy to be present for the birth of her beautiful daughter. But, in the back of my mind was an alarm that I was breaking down.

Each new day brought with it more weakness and fatigue. Performing the basic tasks of running a household was too much for me. Occasionally, I would feel well enough to do some light housework but was far from where I wanted to be with my health and energy level. Two weeks after my sister's baby was born I was still extremely exhausted, so I decided to try a new bottle of a liquid B12 complex that we had recently started carrying at the herb store we owned. Glancing at the directions on the bottle, I poured one-fourth a cup and drank it down. Within fifteen minutes there was a sharp gripping in my gut. I felt nausea and severe cramping. My neck was hot and pressure began to build up in my head. Grabbing the bottle and reading the directions again, I realized the proper dosage was one-fourth a teaspoon. How could I make such an error? Owning an herb store, I was always careful about dosage. But even with this high of dose, I shouldn't have had such a severe reaction. The pain in my gut was getting worse and fearing that I had poisoned myself, I thrust my fingers toward the back of my throat and repeatedly vomited until my stomach was empty. Yet the intensity of pain only increased. Gripping my midsection in the fetal position on my bedroom floor, I became stiflingly hot. I made my way outside to my back lawn for some fresh air. Unable to stand up, I continued crawling around on all fours, belching and heaving with no relief from the sharp pain in my abdomen.

That evening, I began having intense stomach spasms that lasted for several hours with bursts of sharp cramping and abdominal pain. By morning, I was incredibly weak. Within hours the cycle of stomach spasms and gripping in my gut came on with greater intensity and continued for an additional eight hours. This cycle repeated for several days with no relief. Fearing for my life, I finally told my husband that I needed to go to the emergency room. Scott spent years as a medical doctor and had been utilizing his knowledge in this area to monitor me. He was hesitant to go the medical route because he knew there was nothing more that the emergency room doctors could provide than what we were already doing at home. But I felt we needed to go in. When we arrived at the ER, they ran some blood tests and lab work, concluding nothing more than gastritis. How could they not see how much pain I was in? I was released and sent home. I felt vulnerable and desperate for help. Hour after hour, I became weaker and weaker.

The next day, I was too weak to walk so Scott carried me out to the living room couch for a change in scenery. With an open layout connected to the kitchen, I could watch the activity of my brother's family and my own going about their day. Scott later walked into the kitchen to refill his coffee before heading into work. I called out to him for a glass of water. It was as if he heard nothing. I was less than ten feet away from him and speaking as loudly as possible with no response. He quickly went out the door to work. I assumed that he was in a hurry and thought that I was asleep. But each person that came in that day had no response to my calls. When I did finally have the attention of others they would lean their ear toward my mouth and ask me to repeat what I was saying because they couldn't understand me. It took every ounce of my energy to say a few words. I was speaking as loudly and clearly as I could and no one understood anything I was saying. Within a few moments I was forced to give up, defeated and unheard, and I drifted back to sleep.

The following evening, I was alone in my bed. There was a gentle lifting sensation from my core and then suddenly I was out of my body, standing at the foot of my bed with a soft glow around me. I was staring at my frail body in bed, the thick brown comforter pulled up around my neck. My hair was disheveled from my restlessness and I could see that my facial expression was still tense from the severe pain. I felt immediate compassion for the weakened state that my body appeared to be in, but I was finally free of pain. Relief and gratitude washed over me as I glanced over to the clock on my dresser then back toward the lifeless body lying in bed. Being a mother conditioned me to check the time as if to measure whether my children were in need of me soon.

The sound of Scott's laughter down the hall caught my attention and instantly I was standing in the living room. Scott was watching *The Simpsons* on TV, with Cloie snuggled up against him and Sofie playing with a few of her toys on the floor at his feet. I was annoyed that he was letting our young girls watch the show with him as I was always trying to protect their innocent minds. Since they were only seven and nine years old, I felt that the adult humor was inappropriate for them.

I was hyperaware of everything and yet, they were completely unaware that I was standing there. I wanted to join them. I wanted to tell my husband to change the channel to a more age-appropriate show but I knew they would not hear me. Simultaneously, I could feel the expanse of my love for them as I watched their beautiful faces.

In an instant, we were no longer in my family room but on a long clearly marked pathway. Scott was sitting on a large rock at the top of the path with Sofie on his lap, Cloie to his left, then Sharlie and Audrie. On Scott's right was Danyen and beside him were my five stepchildren. I was grateful to see them all together as a family unit but incredibly confused as to why we were there. I was moving away from them and being pulled by an unknown source yet not feeling the ground below me. I locked eyes with Scott first. I heard him say, "I love you, babe; I will be okay," and watched tears stream down his face. "Okay with what? What are you talking about?" I turned my attention to my oldest daughter, Sharlie, who was sobbing uncontrollably but managed to also say that she would be okay. Then to my second daughter, Audrie. She was maintaining her strong composure and was there with her boyfriend who was standing behind her with his arms comforting her. She looked at me and said, "Mom, it's okay, I will be alright too." This exchange continued with my son Danyen, who also said that he would be okay. Cloie could hardly speak through her crying but managed to say, "I will be okay, Mommy," then buried her head into Sharlie's chest. And then sweet Sofie. Seeing shock in her eyes, I could feel that the pain was overwhelming her and all that she could do was to cling tight to her father. I wanted to comfort her and tell her that I'm right here and I'm not going anywhere, yet the force was stronger than I was—it continued pulling me further away from my family. I was in a state of confusion. Why are we on this path? Why do they all keep telling me that they are okay? I'm not okay. I don't want to leave you; I want to be with you. Why isn't anyone stopping me?

As I continued further on the path my mother, father, and siblings were standing together. Although my parents divorced when I was nine years old, they remained on friendly terms with one another. They stood there comforting each other with the loss of their daughter but even they didn't stop me from moving forward. My mom and I locked eyes. I knew she loved me very much and it pained her to see me go. Why wasn't she stopping me? I then passed by my siblings and their families. Behind my immediate family were members of my extended family—aunts, uncles, and cousins—and further behind them were friends and different people in my life. It was as though every person that would be impacted by my dying was there to tell me that they would be okay without me. They all repeated the same thing to me. "We will be okay." No one pleaded with me to stay or told me that I would be missed. No one tried to stop me. There was no conversation, just a simple statement from each person that I loved: "I will be okay," as I involuntarily continued moving forward into the unknown and away from my family.

At the end of the path I could see in front of me a dark building with sharp spires on the roof. There was a wrought iron fence around it with a dilapidated yard that consisted of a dead tree in the front right corner and lifeless bushes along the iron gate. Black ravens were perched on top of the building staring down at me as I approached. It reminded me of a classic haunted mansion scenario that you would see in a movie and didn't resemble anything that I imagined of the spirit realm. My natural inclination in life was to avoid anything scary. I hated scary movies and refused to go to any haunted house during Halloween, but upon seeing this building, I did not feel fearful in any way. There was a calm that washed over me as an observer of what I was experiencing.

Astonishingly, as I arrived at the gate entrance, the dark building began to transfigure. The dead, yellow grass began to show a vibrant green while the tree and bushes came alive with vivid green leaves. The building transformed from a cold, dark space to one that illuminated light. The sharp spires on the roof rounded. Even the ravens transformed into white doves. I could feel the vibration of love emanating from everything. Before me was a completely transfigured place of beautiful golden light. Three beautiful entities welcomed me as I stepped through the threshold. There was a crystalline, warm glow that illuminated from their cores. They were all similar in size and form and their brightness was so magnificent that it prevented me from making out any specific markings to differentiate one from another. I could feel that they loved me very much and that their knowledge was infinite—as was their love for humanity.

These three entities seemed to oversee this specific area. They informed me that my soul was in transition and that my physical body was very ill. Until this point, although I knew my physical body remained in my bedroom, I had been moving through this experience as if I were still in physical form. By all accounts, I looked exactly as I did only moments before. The entities smiled at me and I felt a gentle release and looked down as my outer self dropped away from me, landing like a crumpled-up outfit on the floor. It felt bizarre to see my body lying on the floor free of all structure and form. At this time, I noticed that I also illuminated the same light and was of the same form as each of these magnificent entities of light before me.

Three more illuminated entities appeared. Two of them gently picked up my discarded shell of a body while the third entity, who entered carrying a large bowl of crystal water, began washing it with a soft crystal sponge. The original three entities described to me that there are many layers to each embodiment of an individual and while my physical body was lying in bed at home, I was, at this point, still attached to that body via a chord of life. The body that was now being washed with the crystal water was another layer of my being. They explained to me that the entities were washing me to assist in the healing of my body, telling me that my physical body was very weak and severely damaged. I asked them why I was there and why my family didn't try to stop me from moving forward. I was told that I had left my body due to the extreme trauma of illness and that my soul was being drawn home, back to God. They also told me that my family didn't try to stop me because their consciousness was not prepared for me to die and, on a conscious level, they were all unaware that I was crossing over. The path where I saw my family was my soul's expression of my journey home and I was shown the people in my life as a reminder of the impact I had on them.

The entities then walked me toward three large altars, each holding a unique statue of gold and other precious metals. It appeared that each altar was a symbolic representation of a spiritual gift that they were bestowing to me. Behind the three altars was a darkened passageway that seemed to be a barrier between the physical and spiritual worlds. Stopping at the base of the first altar, which was the brightest and tallest, I was told that I was not to go any further on this path for now. Somehow, I knew that if they showed me the wonders and beauty of what lie beyond these statues that I would not return to my family. I understood that it was important to keep my attention there, knowing that if more of the mystery of the spirit realm was revealed to me it would forever hold my attention captive.

One of the entities then said to me, "You are being given three gifts. The first one is the gift of sight." Instantly, many images appeared before me simultaneously. I watched multiple video clips showing my husband and children and the lives they would live without me. I saw everything. How my husband became so despondent in his grief that he focused his attention on work to stay busy and removed himself from family gatherings, living the rest of his life in loneliness, surrounded by clutter and shutting out the world around him. How my sisters and mother reached out to Scott, trying to include him in family events but they reminded him too much of me so he distanced himself. How my oldest daughter, Sharlie, moved back home to raise her two younger sisters, which prevented her from meeting the person that she would have married. How my siblings tried to make sense of what took place. How at Audrie's wedding to her then-boyfriend, her heart ached to share her wedding day with me. How my son lived with his father for two more years then moved away from the family that loved him, leaving him feeling lost in the world. How Sharlie and Cloie would have long conversations about what they remembered about me until they laughed or cried. How Cloie struggled to fit in with any of her peers because none of them understood the void of not having a mother.

Chapter 1 - The Journey

It saddened me to watch glimpses of each of them growing up and the heartache that they were forced to experience. But they, as do most people who suffer loss, eventually moved on and truly did seem to be okay, just as they told me on the path. I was then showed images of my youngest daughter, Sofie. The trauma of losing me hit her the hardest. I saw that although my older children were severely affected by the loss of their mother, they would manage and were able to continue on with their lives. Sofie, though, did not have the emotional resilience to recover from the trauma of my death.

The entities told me that Sharlie and Cloie had each other to lean on and created a special bond for healing and strength. Audrie had the support of the man who would become her husband and her friends. Danyen remained reserved but had resiliency. The entities made it clear that Sofie would not live out her life purpose without me. They did not share with me what her purpose was but expressed that I was an integral part of that purpose. When they showed me images of her life, I could see that she did not progress: she was frozen in trauma.

Seeing the damage that my death would cause to Sofie shocked and saddened me. I turned toward the entities of light and said to them, "I have to go back. Sofie needs me."

In an instant, I was back in my bed. Back in the density of my physical body and back in unimaginable pain. There was no longer a glow in my room. It was dark and lonely, but I had a passion inside of me to heal. I could hear the TV still on down the hall. I could hear that *The Simpsons* was over, but knew that the battle for my life had just commenced. I glanced over at the clock again and saw that eight minutes had passed since I left my body. In the other dimension, it was timeless.

I began my battle to stay in my body. I needed to heal and to raise my family. Sofie did need me, but so did Cloie and Scott, and the rest of my family. I lifted my hands in front of my face. No longer emanating golden light, they now appeared lifeless and weak. I gently touched them to the stomach that hurt so badly, quietly saying to myself, "Please God, let me heal."

My body was so weak that I still didn't have the strength to talk. Even if I wanted to share with my family what just took place I didn't have the energy to do so. Besides, I was sure there would be many questions that I didn't have the answers to. My sympathetic nervous system was still on high alert, and shakes reverberated through my body. My eyes felt strained and heavy. I kept gently stroking my hands across the different parts of my body and internally repeating to myself, "I choose to live. I choose to live."

I knew that Scott would soon bring the girls into our room to circle around me for our nightly family prayer. This was a ritual that he maintained. When they came in, Sofie stood at my right side with Scott and Cloie next to her. I was so weak and in such deep pain that I could scarcely respond to Scott holding my hand. With no voice to share what had just taken place, I remained quiet. Scott prayed for my healing and for comforting for our family. He prayed for our children to be protected and to know that they were loved. When he finished the prayer, Sofie leaned in and laid her sweet face against mine. I could feel her warmth on my cheek as she whispered in my ear, "I need you, Mommy." My heart ached. I desperately wanted to respond to her. "I know, baby. I am here with you. I promise to never leave you. I promise to heal."

In that moment, my prayers deepened further and so did my determination to keep those promises that were left unsaid as the soft cascade of tears streamed down my face and pooled into my ears. My daughter needed me, and I needed to live.

Oh, God. Please help me live.

CHAPTER 2

Convalescence

My healing journey had begun but I was still deep in pain and fear. In the days following my experience, I didn't have the physical strength to sit up for very long and needed someone to assist me walking to the bathroom or moving from one room to another. The pain in my abdomen was intense every moment. When asked how I was feeling, the only answer that I could give was on a pain scale of 1 to 10, my body was a level 27. My nerves were raw and burned as if on fire. My muscles ached from being held in a state of constant tension. I would intuitively wrap my arms protectively around my abdomen for an added sense of security, knowing that anything that could potentially touch my stomach would feel like a dull punch to the gut. My internal body temperature felt like I was in a meat locker 24/7. Even months later, during the heat of the summer, which was often over one hundred degrees Fahrenheit, I continuously felt chilled. I kept a comforter and blanket layered around me and always held a heating pad gingerly over my belly, often removing the pad cover to get maximum heat transfer through my pajamas.

Any form of heat on my skin was soothing and dulled the internal pain. When I showered, I kept the water as hot as my skin could handle to relax my over-exerted nerves. I was chronically bloated and the heat comforted my achy body and swollen belly. Every night I tried to calm my system by focusing on my breathing and meditating, but my mind would race out of control. Slowing down my breathing only increased my attention on my abdomen and would begin a series of panic attacks. As the sun went down night after night my anxiety would flare up, knowing I would have to endure another sleepless night of shaking, vomiting, and diarrhea. I was exhausted from the sleep deprivation and felt desperate for help.

I slipped in and out of wakefulness each day, trying to hold my body in perfect stillness through waking and sleeping. The slightest movement would send my system into uncontrolled shaking, deeper pain, and increased nausea. It took effort to chew any food. Holding the weight of my head upright was even too much to bear. Sitting up to eat something, I would often need to prop my elbow on the kitchen table and lean my head into the palm of my hand to carry the extra burden of the weight of my head. Even sipping water was too much for my stomach to tolerate, which left me severely dehydrated.

In that first two weeks after I resolved to fight for my life and heal, I would often stare at the wrinkled skin on my hands and arms, marveling how old they looked from the dehydration. From using the toilet, it was clear that the few items that I managed to eat left my body completely undigested. I would often make my way back to bed from the bathroom and pause to see my image in front of the large mirror above the bathroom sink. My body looked so fragile and the skin hung from my face and arms. My hair was falling out and I could see a deep and prominent groove down the center of my tongue, which I knew in Ayurvedic medicine was considered an indication of poor digestion. Sighing in resignation, I would make my way back to my bed.

My mother would come over to my home and cook down brown rice, which she then blended to a liquid form. She would sit beside me and spoon baby-size portions into my mouth, patiently waiting for my strained efforts to swallow. She would prepare warm tea with ginger and honey to soothe my nausea, holding the straw against my lips since I lacked the strength necessary to lift my head enough to keep tea from spilling down my chin. The rare opportunity of deep sleep was provided when my mother would gently massage my limbs, allowing my muscles to relax and my nervous system to calm.

Chapter 2 - Convalescence

From the very beginning of my illness, I had reached out to a variety of healers and practitioners with little if any noticeable results. I was fortunate enough to have access to a multitude of naturopaths, doctors, healers, and therapists due to my husband's connections in the healing field. Scott is a spiritual intuitive with a phenomenal gift of intuition. He is also a former medical doctor and public speaker, who left allopathic medicine to expand into other fields of healing. Clients often appreciated the combination of his medical background and his spiritual insight. Although he no longer diagnosed disease he would intuitively communicate with spiritual guides and often provided life-changing insight to clients across the country. Yet he too had no answers for me.

While I did sometimes receive a test result that pointed toward a small part of what was happening in my body, I received no clear answers or feedback that left me with a sense of how I needed to proceed. I continued, in pain, still seeking, not knowing how I could make it go away.

Christmas that year arrived with very little fanfare. Thankfully, with the few items that I purchased earlier in the year, our children still had some semblance of the holiday. Scott helped me into the living room to interact with my family from the couch and watch them open their gifts. I still hadn't shared with any of them what had happened to me only nine days earlier. I knew that if I told my children in my weakened state, it would only scare them more. And, besides, I didn't have the physical strength to talk enough to share the whole experience, let alone answer any questions that anyone might have after hearing the details. I decided to wait for now and just enjoy my family as much as I could. I watched them open gifts and visit with one another, trying to put on a slight smile each time one of them would look over to me with concern in their eyes.

I sat with them for two hours and then had Scott and Danyen help me back to bed. My mind wandered to the possibility of how this day may have been had I not come back—it would have been the first of many Christmases tainted with loss and grief for my children. But, I was alive and grateful that my children were with me. I fell asleep to the sounds of my family down the hall.

Two weeks passed and school was back in session. I still hadn't told Scott of my experience. Partly because the act of talking took more energy than I could spare, and it was still quite a challenge in my weakened state, but also because it was still difficult to wrap my mind around what I experienced. How close I had been to dying and leaving my family. I was emotional and frightened of what could have been and yet I was also feeling such an urgency around getting out of pain. I was willing to do nearly anything to alleviate my suffering, even if it meant death. Crossing over to the other side had expanded my consciousness to the reality that everything really is okay. I recalled the images shown to me of how my children and husband experienced deep grief in losing me, yet over time eventually created a new normal in their individual lives. But, my mind held fast to the images of Sofie not fulfilling her life purpose.

Scott was tired and weighed down by the extra responsibility of running the home and parenting alone, which only layered with the fear of losing his wife, the guilt that he couldn't fix me, and the responsibilities of running a business. Although he never complained about his struggles, knowing that mine were much more intense, the toll on him was visible. I knew it was time to summon all the energy I had and share my experience.

Like any other marriage, we had endured many challenges and having my husband hold me often provided peace when I felt fear or frustration. Although I didn't feel these emotions at this point, I knew that he did and needed my presence as much as I needed his. I asked him to lie down beside me. I wanted to feel his warmth and remember what it felt like to have bedroom talk with the person that I loved so much. Our intimacy had shifted away from lovemaking, limiting connection in bed to holding hands as we drifted to sleep each night. It saddened me that I couldn't fulfill his needs any more than he could fulfill mine. When I allowed my mind to wander back into the life that already felt so far away, I smiled, recalling our passion and fun. We were a perfect match in the bedroom. Since becoming ill, I didn't have the capacity to share my body with my husband, but I needed to share with him the sacred experience of near death.

It was too painful for me to turn to my side and face him but I needed to see his face and connect with him while I shared what I experienced. I told him every detail while he stared at me, transfixed by what he was hearing. I started to cry when I told him what I saw about him living without me. He nodded in agreement, recognizing his personality. As we spoke, we acknowledged that not only had I been living in a constant state of survival, but so had my family. My children could see that I was very sick and in tremendous pain. We were all fearful of the "what ifs" and felt helpless and uncertain of our family's future. Scott and I both agreed to not share my experience with our young children yet, knowing that it would frighten them even more.

It was challenging for me and our children without my active, involved presence in their everyday activities. I had missed every school event in the first half of the school year. Toward the end of January, Cloie had a choir concert and I was determined to make it. I remembered being in my third-grade program and looking out into the school auditorium, hoping to lock eyes with my mother but realizing she wasn't there, finding out later that her boss hadn't let her off work to attend. I was determined to not let Cloie feel that same disappointment I felt so many years before.

The afternoon of her concert, Cloie arrived home from school and came in to see if I was going to her concert as I had promised. How could I tell her that I had been shaking all day? That the nausea was so extreme that even the slightest movement felt as if I would be sent over the edge? I didn't want the guilt of letting down my daughter, and assured her that I would be there.

Scott carried me to the car and then into the auditorium. I felt vulnerable and humiliated that other families were staring at us as we arrived. I felt ashamed and helpless, and, also sad that I allowed myself to feel shame when I was doing everything I could to heal, continuing to seek answers and try anything I thought might help. I didn't want Cloie's peers to judge her for her mother's weakness. Lacking the physical strength to sit up right, I asked Scott to lay me down between two rows toward the back of the auditorium. The concrete floor was hard and cold and the bolts holding the chairs in place were pressing against me. I worried that I would be stepped on if someone unknowingly came seeking an empty seat in the darkened room.

On the floor in the auditorium, I felt angry that I was still sick, scared that it would never end, guilty that my daughter had to fix her own hair, and battling my bruised ego for appearing weak to others. I had spent my life trying to prove to the world that I could do what I set my mind to do. And now, I couldn't even sit upright. I closed my eyes, imagining Cloie in her dress. Attuning my ears to the sound of her voice, and reminding myself that even though she knew that I was there, she would not be able to scan the audience and lock eyes on her mother. I continued to layer the emotional pain of not being there in the manner that my daughter hoped for with the physical pain that my body was feeling.

That night, my determination to heal only increased. Scott felt helpless in his attempts to assist me in healing and I felt more and more desperate. Intuitively, Scott knew that he needed to take me away from my environment so that I could start the healing process. He booked us a flight to Hawaii on the island of Kauai. Leaning on Scott for support I mustered up all the physical strength that I could and somehow managed to walk onto the plane, concerned that a flight attendant would stop me from flying if they noticed my weakened state. The fresh island air strengthened and revitalized me and I was hopeful that we were being directed to the right people for help. We arrived at the Wyndham resort and joined the other guests in the main lobby for a welcome event where the resort staff shared island activities and a light dinner. I believe it was fate that we ended up right next to the person that was going to help me.

During the welcome event, I sat on the large overstuffed leather chair watching the other guests mingle about. They all looked so normal, laughing over glasses of wine and delicate appetizers. I wanted to connect with others there but didn't feel it to be possible in that moment, since no one around me showed evidence of having any connection to what I was going through. I watched others enjoying their food and not even being conscious of what they were putting in their mouths. It didn't matter because nothing they were eating was going to cause them any pain.

I was eating a light salad and praying to not have a reaction to the food when a woman sat next to me and began making small chat. She asked me where we were from. "Utah," I replied. She then asked if we had been to this island before and I explained that I had been to Oahu and the Big Island a few times each but this was my first time on Kauai. Still prodding, she asked me why we came to this island. Not knowing how much I dared to share with a total stranger, I explained that I had been quite ill and that my husband brought me here to heal. She held her attention on my face. I could feel her deep blue eyes penetrating through me as she looked at me with compassion and kindness. She exuded truth and wisdom from her heart. Taking a few slow deep breaths, her eyes remained transfixed on me. Internally, I wondered if I had shared too much. People come to Hawaii as a vacation and to let go of stress, not to rescue a complete stranger from illness. But then she lovingly stated, "I feel that I am supposed to help you on your healing journey."

She told me that her name was Sharon Forrest and that she did energy healing work. I also learned that she was an ordained minister and a naturopathic physician and possessed many other gifts. By this time Scott had joined the conversation, along with Sharon's friend that had traveled with her. I have always believed in energy healers and fully anticipate that God will place the right person in your path when you are ready. We arranged to meet the following morning in her condo at the resort.

The next morning, Scott and I were met at the door by her friend, who had brought Sharon on vacation as a respite from her heavy workload as a healer and from running orphanages in Peru. The four of us sat at the little round table in the kitchen and Sharon explained that when the spirit was ready to begin the healing work a cross would appear on her pointer finger and we could begin. We visited for another fifteen to twenty minutes and during that time, I didn't take my eyes off her finger. I had no idea what to anticipate but whatever it was, I wasn't going to miss it.

When it was time to begin, a red cross appeared on her finger just as she had said it would. With excited anticipation, the four of us went into the living room where they had moved the furniture to accommodate my session. Sharon's friend, the designated scribe, sat with Scott on the couch while I sat on a dining room chair that had been placed at the edge of the room for me. Sharon explained that they needed the space to be clear to protect me from injuring myself during the healing experience. She said that I would likely end up on the floor but that she would guide me and protect me from hurting myself. She also explained how it was common for people to scream or yell during their session. I am not one to create drama and was certain that I would not be one of those people.

Sharon placed her hands on my head. I could feel a warm energy penetrating from her hands and very soon, my body began to sway in a gentle circular motion. Within a few moments, Sharon braced my body as I surrendered and she supported me as I dropped to the carpeted floor and through a vortex of time and space. In my mind's eye, I was instantly transported to the final hours of a past life where I had been poisoned and died. The details were incredibly clear and the images felt so real. All my senses were enhanced. I could smell and taste and hear everything around me. It was as real as life is today. I was the observer of the life experience and the person experiencing the life. In this dual time, it felt like a virtual reality experience where I resided in one realm with others around me, but was simultaneously fully engaged in a whole other experience. I could feel the energy of cramping and retching. I could feel the fear of death run through me. I had an acute awareness of my senses being enhanced—the awareness of sharp pains from my insides being destroyed. Then suddenly it was over and I was hovering over the body. Then I was once again fully present, back in my physical body, feeling the soft carpet beneath me. A sense of calm washed over me and I was quiet and peaceful.

I could see nothing but the void around me for a few moments, then suddenly, and without notice, again I was transported to another past life. Now I was a man, engaged in a brawl with another man. Suddenly, I was stabbed in the throat with a sharp blade. I felt shock and the memory of searing pain in my neck, but without the physical sensation of pain. I could feel my mouth fill up with blood and taste the warm liquid pooling in the back of my throat causing me to choke. In the present realm, I began choking and coughing violently and then as before, there was a sudden end to the virtual life experience as that body died. And then again, quiet.

In another experience, I lived in the wild and could feel the vines whipping my legs as I ran through the dense foliage. It was like being an actor in a blockbuster movie and an audience member all at once. This lifetime was very primitive and harsh. I could feel my heart race as I ran in fear for my life, but lacked the consciousness of respect for human life. It was survival of the fittest. Either kill or be killed, and I had met my match. Death was quickly approaching as I could not outrun my opponent. Weapons for battle and for hunting had been constructed using sharpened stones bound by twine to spears. I knew that the tips of these weapons were dipped in a concoction used to cause paralysis of the victim upon impact. I jolted sharply as I felt the impact pierce my right lower back, hitting my head hard against the ground floor. I was conscious as my assailant removed the spear and pierced me again for good measure. And then felt a quiet calm.

One of the more intense experiences was a lifetime where I had been wrongly accused of a crime I did not commit. I was chained and shackled at my wrists and ankles and left to die in a damp and dark dungeon. I was provided rotting scraps of food and unclean water, held bound against the brick wall by stones that anchored my chains. This specific incident was horrific and unjust. I cried out to be rescued and made countless attempts to free my limbs from bondage, tightly grasping one hand over the other wrist and pulling with intense force. Much like a Chinese finger trap toy, the harder I pulled, the tighter my bonds became. This life showed years of bondage and false imprisonment. (This helped explain to me why in my current life I cannot tolerate a watch or bracelet around my wrists-they always feel too confining.)

The cycle of the apex of each life, death, and then peace repeated for four hours. Each experience as vivid and real as the one before. My senses were alive to the colors and images in each environment. The smells were rich and my emotions were heightened and attuned to the climax of each life.

The only sensation that I didn't feel was pain. Even when I was aware of the gripping in my gut, the stabbing of a blade, the pounding of my heart in my chest, or the pressures of childbirth, there was a pressure in these areas of my body but no pain. In one of these experiences, I was giving birth to a beautiful baby girl. My physical body was reacting to the contractions and I could feel myself bear down and push with the sensation of my cervix expanding and the baby pushing through the tight opening of the birth canal, but without the physical pain. Suddenly, my attention was brought back to being on the carpeted floor due to a strong odor of blood and I could feel the warmth running down my legs and pooling beneath me. I felt embarrassed and concerned that I had literally bled all over the creamy white carpet of the condo. With my eyes closed, I asked if we could stop the session so that I could go to the bathroom and clean up the blood before I ruin the carpet. Although everyone in the room could also smell the blood, there was no blood present. I was shocked when I opened my eyes to confirm this even though the strong scent of blood was burning my nostrils. I ran my hands down my inner thighs and could feel the blend of two worlds. My yoga pants were dry, but I could still feel the warm and wet from the blood of a previous existence. I knew I had hemorrhaged while giving birth in that life and died.

Closing my eyes again, I was immediately transported to a life where I was in a large control room with advanced computer systems. The walls were made of glass and I could see the beautiful overgrown foliage outside. I was part of a team that was experimenting with technology that was new in development. We were no match for the magnitude of power that was being harnessed, and which ultimately contributed to the destruction of our civilization. In the present, I began frantically speaking tongues and my hand was banging in a rhythmic manner similar to Morse code on the carpeted floor. In my past life experience,

I was watching mass destruction and the ending of thousands, if not millions of lives. I was sending the message: Abort! Abort! Abort! There was panic in my breathing as I witnessed a huge explosion and then it was over. I had the inner knowing that this experience took place on Atlantis, but many of the other experiences were of no consequence to humanity at large and affected only my limited environment.

I experienced lifetimes in jungle tribes and in harsh mountain winters. I lived through bleak poverty and through famine. I died from bullet wounds and stabbings, from being burned at the stake, and from hangings. Each of these lifetimes carried a trauma that I needed to release so that I could heal my body in my current life.

When we completed the session, I felt like I was coming out of a deep trance. There was a lightness in my body that I hadn't felt before. It was all so surreal. I regained more of my strength and vitality and was very grateful. Scott and I spent the rest of the week taking gentle strolls on the beach and resting. I felt hope that healing was taking place. Little did I know, I still had a long road ahead of me.

We returned home, and although I had felt a momentary improvement in my health while in Hawaii, returning to my responsibilities pulled me back into my same patterns, beliefs, and behaviors. My nervous system was still raw and my digestion and abdomen were weak and severely damaged. I would start to feel more strength and push myself to do a little more activity, only to end up back in bed for two or three days.

Severe stomach pain continued to be my daily companion and my arms continued to cradle my abdomen. I would lie awake for hours each night because the pain was so severe. My nerves were on constant alert and I felt completely burned out. Searing sensations ran through my limbs and back. During the day, I would doze in and out from absolute exhaustion. On the nights that I could sleep for a few hours I often woke up with a hope that it was all a bad dream. Then once fully conscious and before I moved any part of my body, I would pray that "today is the day that I will feel better" only to have that dashed away with more nausea and pain. Each moment that passed left me with fear that I would have to endure another moment. When I thought that I could not physically handle one second more I would feel panic rush through me. My mind continually cried out in protest: I can't do this! Why am I going through this pain? When will this nightmare end?

Days bled into weeks and then months. I longed for the life that I once lived, working out at the gym and enjoying occasional lunch dates with friends. In the beginning of my illness, friends would occasionally send me a text message of, "Hey, haven't seen you in a while. Want to get together for lunch?" I was grateful that people remembered that I was no longer showing up in the outside world, but feared that they would ask me about my health. I didn't have the answers and believed if others were aware of how truly ill I was, they would question my sanity as to why I wasn't in the hospital. Intuitively, I knew that I would not have healed in the hospital. Although I was looking for answers everywhere I could, I started having a sense that my healing would need to come from within.

I was in hibernation from life. I felt as though everyone else around me continued to live their lives as normally as possible while I was in stasis. Even though my brother and his family were still living in our basement and my husband and children were in the home, much of the time I was alone in my room with my sweet and loyal cocker spaniel, Angel. She diligently stayed on the floor beside me, only getting up when she saw me shifting. She watched me cautiously but was always present. Angel stayed with me the entire year of 2013 through my healing process. A year after my near-death experience she suddenly developed multiple tumors and died shortly after. Many of us believed that she assisted my healing and somehow took some of the energetic burden that my body was carrying. I felt immense grief in her passing but will be eternally grateful that she was with me when I needed a friend.

I was recognizing that the effects of illness were not limited to feeling physical pain, but also included a great deal of emotional weight, including fear and trauma.

Chapter 2 - Convalescence

When I was fifteen, I traveled with my grandparents to Canada. I was there for the summer to assist my grandfather, who was building my aunt's home. I loved spending time with my cousins in the fresh mountain air and enjoyed being productive. I wasn't one to shy away from work. While we were there, however, I came down with such a horrible bout of the stomach flu, I couldn't even keep down water. I felt weak and dehydrated from vomiting so much and was either on the bathroom floor, wrapped around the toilet bowl, or on the couch huddled in a ball to keep warm. I loved my grandmother but she was a strict warden and firmly believed that only lazy people stayed in bed when they felt under the weather. Compassion was not her strong suit.

On the morning of the second day I sat huddled in a blanket at the kitchen table sipping hot ginger tea that my Aunt Lorna made for me, hoping to keep some liquids down. When my grandmother came around the corner she gave me a sharp blow to the top of my head with her knuckle. She demanded that I get up and work it off, reminding me that I was here to help and was not going to waste my aunt's time making me tea. She made it clear that I was not going to be a louse, sleeping on the couch while others were out working. The shock and intensity of that hit on my head still haunts me today. I had no choice but to get up and go outside, presumably to work. Thankfully, my cousins took pity on me and hid me in an area of the property that wasn't visible from the house. I sat on the chilly damp grass, cradling my stomach and rubbing the top of my head, afraid of being caught and even more afraid of being hit again. That incident had a profound effect over me and branded into my subconscious the desire to never look weak and to work as hard as I could to avoid punishment.

Here I was again, ill and still in bed with no further information as to why. When someone got word that I was still sick, they often followed with the standard questions: Why are you still sick? Why aren't you in the hospital? Why hasn't your husband healed you? To be confronted with someone else demanding answers when they weren't part of the day-to-day survival was too much for me to bear.

My husband was one of many healers that tried to help me. He and

I were both mystified as to why healing hadn't taken place. This strained our relationship because he had helped thousands of people, yet was unable to provide me with answers. Many healers will confirm that to work on someone so close to you is quite challenging—too deep in the forest to see the trees.

I felt isolated and abandoned by the outside world and my body. Scrolling through others' Facebook posts or watching television momentarily distracted me from my own world, but emotions of jealousy and envy would often show up when I would see posts of lives that other people were living while I was miserable in bed.

Being alone with my thoughts, I often looked for a deeper understanding. I feared that I wasn't praying correctly, rationalizing that if I had stronger faith or my thoughts were pure then God would deem me worthy of assistance and healing. I believed the rest of the world around me knew the secrets of vitality and there was some conspiracy that I wasn't privy to where they refused to share with me the secrets to healing. I felt guilty that I was failing my family and that I would die having accomplished nothing of value. When Scott would come home from work I would beg him to give me answers as to what was going on within me. He was compassionate with words and yet his eyes showed helplessness. He would tell me that every time he prayed for answers for my healing the only answer that he intuitively heard was that this was my journey, and I needed to look within for my healing. This left me with a deeper sense of feeling abandoned and not supported. I rationalized that I spent my life taking care of everyone else and now that I was the one in need, no one was answering my call for help. I believed that somewhere out there was my magic cure and I needed to just keep looking until I found it.

There were a few things I did know. I knew that I was reacting to foods but I wasn't sure which ones. I knew that I wasn't digesting much of anything. I knew that I was experiencing horrible pain and I knew that I had a long road ahead of me in my healing process.

When the pain intensified, I became aware that I was energetically detaching from my body and would often want to emotionally escape from the physical experience because it was too difficult for me to handle. I replayed my near-death experience in my head repeatedly and wrote often in my journal, looking for some hidden gem that I may have overlooked. I felt confused about the messages given by the entities when they told me that I was given the gift of sight. Sight of what? Was the gift of sight a momentary experience while I was crossed over, where I was allowed to see my family live without me, or was it a gift that I would return with in this life that needed to be strengthened? I didn't feel that having any of the knowledge provided to me was going to help we with the mess that I was in. Why didn't they just tell me how I screwed up in life and what I needed to do to fix it? And, what were the other two gifts that were represented by the remaining two altars? Did I screw that up too, by leaving too soon before they had a chance to tell me what those were? Why didn't I ask more questions about God and my purpose?

There were days that I felt marginally well but these would often be followed by days of feeling extreme weakness, pain, and fatigue. During one of these bouts in bed, feeling as though I had depleted every avenue of information about healing that I could find in the Western world, I decided to extend my reach to my dear friend Jennifer Winfield, in Australia. I sent a text message to her briefly explaining my current situation in hope that she was privy to some aboriginal healing practice or possibly knew of any wisdom that would assist me in rebuilding my nervous system and digestive system. Within a few hours my phone lit up with her incoming message, which read, *"As you know, kids are a wonderful journey but they do drain every ounce of energy in our systems and we work on overload much of the time. Sometimes these illnesses are a reminder for us to self-care but also of our own mortality and vulnerability. It will pass. Enjoy the rest...read and catch up on uplifting movies, documentaries, or TV series. Convalescing is a word we no longer use yet with the speed in which the Western culture shakes us about makes it a much-needed one. We all require quiet time to grow internally and process our lives. Drop into the fear and worry and watch it transform. Sending you much love and healing light."*

Lying in bed, I was transfixed as I repeatedly reread her message to me. My eyes kept going over the word "convalescing." Up until this point I don't think I even knew the accurate definition of that word. I had assumed it had something to do with the elderly since the few times that I heard the word convalescence was in relation to geriatrics. Determined to gain a clearer understanding of the message my friend sent me, I gingerly slithered off my bed and made my way down the hall into my library in search of my Webster's dictionary. The weight of the large book was too much for me in my weakened state and it dropped to the floor. Turning through the pages, I finally came upon the definition of convalescence. It read, "1. gradual recovery after illness 2. the period of such recovery."

It had taken me nearly ten minutes to crawl from my bed to where I was now sitting on the floor, leaning against the bookshelf in my library. Fatigue and emotion washed over me. I felt too weak to even cry but somehow the tears voluntarily streamed down my face. It was as though some force outside of me was giving me permission to be where I was. It kindled within me the awareness that I was not at the beginning or end of my path but immersed deeply within it. This simple but profound insight gave me an opportunity to step back from it all and to perceive my experience from another view. Since I didn't have the strength to crawl back to my room and no one would be home for another few hours, I closed the book and held it close to me as I rested my face against the carpeted floor and wept. I was convalescing and I needed sleep.

Before I was ill, I lived my life very active and for the most part, I enjoyed that. The one downside was that I often pushed myself too hard to the point of exhaustion. On some level, I was hoping that God would one day glance down upon me as I served my family with dedication and deem me worthy of a graduation from the mundane existence that I felt inside of me.

My mind was often pulled back to Jennifer's acknowledgment of the energy we give our children. My children were my everything and I am eternally grateful for each of them. But, as a parent, I had spent years smoldering the fire within me for a greater calling for my soul. I was lost in the shadow of parenthood. Often feeling guilt for wanting more for myself and frustration that I didn't even know what that "more" was. There was no tribe that I belonged to or connecting force with another individual that recognized my hunger. I feared the source of soul nourishment was on lockdown with no sign of reopening any time soon. I quietly longed for someone to give me permission to be selfish with my time and to focus on myself rather than every other person's whim, and now it was granted and I was miserable. Here I was with plentiful time all to myself—but only because I had no capacity to care for the needs of my children, which meant I also had no capacity to find my purpose in life.

Over the next few months I regained enough strength to do some mild housework. I could start a load of laundry or put a few dishes in the dishwasher. On days when I had minimal pain and some energy, I would try to capitalize on the newfound strength and catch up on house cleaning, only to fall back in bed harder the next day. Although I knew that I had zero energy reserves to go beyond my basic needs, and convalescing was what I was doing, there was still ingrained deep within me the language of my grandparents from when I was a teenager: "Get up and work it off." Staying in bed was only perpetuating more of what I didn't want. Guilt.

My body constantly ached from tension and spending days in bed. I would adjust myself several times in a fruitless effort to feel more comfortable, cradling my mid-section just as much for physical relief as emotional comfort. Pregnancy was forever written on my body with stretch marks and excess skin distended to its capacity, emphasizing the lack of muscle tone. The damage to my intestines and my poor digestion had taken their toll, and my response was one of loathing and disgust. I was conscious of the countless times over the years I had caught sight of my profile as I walked past a full-length mirror, my attention instantly pulled toward my stomach. "Stupid fat," I would think. "I hate you."

I had become a first-time mother at the tender age of seventeen in a very Mormon community in southern Utah. The emotional cycle of self-deprecation and shame was heavy throughout my life. What I lacked in self-love, I made up for in busy work and service. I somehow convinced myself that if I couldn't love how I looked then no one else could. Certainly, I was an embarrassment to my husband and children. Determined to demonstrate my value to them, before I became sick, I spent an average of six to eight hours a day cleaning and cooking and serving my family's needs.

My days had become quite different, but my feelings of shame and disgust for my body remained. Due to my illness, I had new sources of dissatisfaction. My face aged from pain. Not only did I feel weak but I looked weak too. My wardrobe consisted of thick flannel pajamas at night and loose yoga pants with a large sweatshirt by day. I couldn't handle anything that put pressure on my abdomen and I was constantly chilled. My once-toned arms were frail and wrinkled, the excess skin sagging in silent resignation.

Now, standing naked before my full-length mirror, I attempted to gaze at the image before me with compassion. I felt that I was separate from the person in the mirror. I longed to hold her and love her and tell her that I was sorry for her pain. I wanted to do what no one else could do for her. To validate that I knew what she was going through. To tell her, "I hear you and you are not alone."

I was finally skinny with a flat belly. Something that I craved for years—but at what cost? My self-value had spiraled even deeper and my need for something to fill the void gnawed at me from within.

There was a missing link and I longed for someone to reassure me that autonomy is encouraged and that to remain a separate entity in a family dynamic is optimal. My desperate belief was that if I did more, and worked harder and faster, then somehow this missing link would appear to me and fill me with a warm glow of completeness.

In the fall of 2013, I was finally strong enough to interact more with my extended family and do some light work around the house. My daughter Audrie got engaged in May of that year. I was tremendously excited for her, yet incredibly fearful that I would not have the strength to help her plan her wedding. I experienced severe panic attacks, fearing that the stress would only put me back in bed.

Chapter 2 - Convalescence

Sadly, the week of her wedding was more challenging than anticipated. My husband's oldest son and his wife delivered a beautiful baby boy with complications. Our precious grandson Knox passed away a few days later—the day before Audrie's wedding. We were overwhelmed with devastation, grief, and helplessness. We longed to hold the hearts of our son and daughter in-law and desired to be fully present for our daughter's wedding, simultaneously. Gratefully, I had the strength to be present at the wedding and the funeral. It was during this time that I felt the presence of grace blanketing our family. There were too many dynamics not to be fully present at each moment. I believe that I was given strength to be present where I was needed and we were held up by a force larger than us. We could feel the prayers and condolences for the loss of our grandson and, also, celebrate in the joy of a family wedding. The small details in life that potentially can drag a person down into a spiral of complaints became inconsequential and the value of life and all the experiences it had to offer was illuminated.

CHAPTER 3

Down the Rabbit Hole

My illness was a daunting task of putting the multiple puzzle pieces together. When I had only a few pieces gathered, they felt nearly useless; my pain still felt like it was never going to end. As I gathered more insight and understanding to the root causes of illness, my experience began to shift. I began to hope. Slowly, I understood what I needed to do, and eventually I knew I could help take others through their own healing journeys.

For most of my adult life, I believed that many of the diseases that we deal with today were simply a combination of nutritional deficiencies and too many environmental toxins in the body. Although these elements are contributors to a breakdown of health, they are certainly not the only components. Other contributing factors for illness in the body are unresolved emotions, parasites, bacteria, radiation, fungus, viruses, stress, body constitution, genetic weakness, and heavy metal toxicity. Each of these can play a role in tipping someone toward disease and illness. Additionally, there are specific experiences that a soul chooses to go through for their individual growth. These experiences can be pinpointed by someone well trained in astrology, specific energy healing techniques, mediumship, or regression therapy.

If a soul chooses to experience growth through disease, illness, or pain for their spiritual development, their life will be set up for those opportunities and conditions to take place—optimizing the potential for learning and expanding in the specific areas desired. While embodied in your current life it would be common to ask, "Why would I choose disease, illness, or pain?" But the reality is that the potential for tremendous expansion in a soul's development outweighs all suffering that would be endured.

Whether or not we see the value in our suffering as we are moving through it, it remains difficult to be in pain. And naturally, we want our suffering to end. In my desperation to heal I tried every modality I could find. Some of the conclusions these modalities offered contradicted assessments from a prior health practitioner, leaving me with more confusion than answers. Most of the time I met with practitioners who could see that I was very ill but had no solutions for my recovery. Often, though, they did help uncover another layer of what was truly going on in my body.

I visited naturopaths and medical doctors. I met with an iridologist, acupuncturist, and NAET practitioner. I tried Eastern medicine and Western medicine and experienced faith healers, energy healers, and trauma release specialists. I had Reiki treatments, massage therapy, and chiropractic adjustments and attended healing retreats and meditation retreats. I provided stool samples, saliva samples, blood samples, and hair samples. I did parasite cleanses, liver detox programs, enemas, and gallbladder flushes. I integrated herbal supplements from Eastern and Western practices while trying homeopathic remedies and applying essential oils. Everything I ate was carefully monitored to be organic and free of any processing chemicals.

Some people told me I was doing too much and others told me I needed to be more vigilant. There were people who told me that I was clearly crying out for attention and others who would cry as they watched me persevere in my weakened state. I experienced past life regressions that provided me with moments of clarity that I was receiving grace, hope, and support. Occasionally, I had dreams of my life in the future where I was vibrant and healthy. I clung to these images like a fistful of sand, drawing hope from them until they spilled from my fingers at the next setback in my health.

My body was like clockwork. My sympathetic nervous system would turn on full alert around 4 p.m. every day and I would shake violently for approximately eight to nine hours. This exhausted every cell in my body. Any food that I had consumed would rush right through me. I later learned that the muscle tremors were a cerebral response to proteins passing into my bloodstream and crossing the blood-brain barrier. My skin and eyes had a slight yellowing which indicated liver infection, and my skin hung from my face and limbs despondently.

As I explored different modalities and visited various practitioners, I discovered some answers as to what was happening to me—test results that indicated a "perfect storm" of challenges my body was facing, which were all a piece of the puzzle. I learned that I had two forms of E. coli, several intestinal parasites, and H-pylori in my gut, contributing to the breaking down of my body's natural defenses and making me susceptible to any foreign substance that entered my body. I had a compromised lining of my intestinal tract which was preventing me from absorbing valuable minerals for optimal health, causing diverticulitis and leaky gut (a condition where, due to an imbalance of microbes in the gut, tiny holes have developed in the intestinal wall allowing proteins to reach the bloodstream). My nervous system was also severely compromised. I had heavy metal toxicity from the improper removal of amalgams and a host of systemic viruses, fungus, and bacteria.

Symptomatically, I knew that my body was in a critical state. Because of my inability to digest valuable nutrients from the food I was eating, my body was forced to pull minerals from within, causing severe muscle fatigue. My sympathetic nervous system was on high alert leaving my adrenals severely depleted and preventing me from entering a parasympathetic state, a state that is of paramount importance for healing and digestion.

How did this happen to me? Looking back, there were certainly many clues that indicated stress in my body. In hindsight, during the previous four to five years, I had been showing signs of imbalance in my health. I experienced joint pain and inflammation and had been under a higher than normal level of stress. I was often bloated and fatigued, feeling low-grade flu-like symptoms and body aches. These symptoms came on slowly, over time, and I adapted to a new normal.

I continued to unfold the layers and step back in time. The previous year, I went to the dentist to have the amalgams removed that had been in my mouth for many years. I trusted that this dental office had the proper ventilation system in place to prevent any excess heavy metals from leaching into my system during the removal, but learned later that their system was not adequate, nor was my body properly prepared to withstand the impact of removal. I now understand the extreme importance in having the pathways of elimination (the kidneys, spleen, and liver) in strong order to process the heavy metal toxins from the body; unfortunately, at the time of removal, my organs were damaged and weak from infection.

Somewhere, I learned to believe that if we live a good life and treat others with respect that we will be blessed and buffered from challenges. That if we do everything right and play by the rules that heartache and pain would not reside in our inner circle. Whose idea was it to instill dreams of good living and rewards of eternal bliss into the consciousness of humanity? This has got to be the biggest heist of all time.

It took me many years to come to this realization. Not because I am bitter and angry. I didn't wake up one day with the jaded epiphany that all is for naught. I absolutely believe in miracles and joy. In fact, God has blessed me with some incredible and miraculous events that cannot be explained at the human level. I marvel at synchronicity and higher purpose. But this realization has released me from the bondage of thinking that I must be doing something wrong if my life is not feeling perfectly blissful and blessed. It feels liberating to know that in the soul's journey of life experiences we will have opportunity to expand our consciousness and awareness through the challenges we have.

We all came to this planet to grow, to learn, to exchange, and to love. Hopefully the "love" part is a huge percentage of the energy that you get to swim around in. If it's not, I'm sorry. I believe that the purpose of this Earth experience is to evolve as an individual and as a species. We show up with gifts or talents that we get to discover on our journey and challenges that are a reminder of what areas in our life we want to put extra attention on. I have the belief that somewhere on God's council sit wise beings of light that decide with us what these challenges are. Let's hope that we weren't left to our own devices to "wing it" and then to be thrown into this world of pain and emotional trauma, just to spend a lifetime trying to get our act together.

The "grow" and "learn" elements of our life experiences sound like an exciting adventure, right? Well, not necessarily and certainly not for me. Why? Because the specific challenges our souls choose to go through will often smack us in the face like a bulldozer on jet fuel. For some, growth can happen through relationships, financial issues, or loss. For me, a great deal of my growth has come through illness. I had studied enough self-help and mindset training to know that for my external world to improve, I needed to make some internal changes but felt confused as to what exactly I needed to change. I felt that my life was a roller coaster that had sped out of control and that I didn't have enough information to put it back on track.

I read health blogs and articles, listened to online summits, and watched documentaries—all in search for answers, but often felt that I was navigating the healing paradigm with very little resources. Over time, it became more and more clear to me that my illness was not going to be healed through traditional means.

I wanted my husband to have the answers. It was common for people who had received an intuitive reading from Scott to tell me, "Your husband saved my life." I witnessed countless readings where his intuition accurately pinpointed a health concern that multiple medical doctors and tests were unable to diagnose. And yet, here I was in front of him every day pleading for answers as to why I was still sick.

I knew this was a lot of pressure on him and he tried to help me. Scott would diligently read into my energy each time I asked, and tell me the same answers. I had a toxic liver due to infection, parasites, and bacteria in my gut, multiple viruses in my nervous system and throughout my body, and heavy metal toxicity, confirming what other tests indicated. He often brought home herbs to heal the intestinal lining as well as supplements for cellular detox, parasite cleansing, and rebuilding the gut, but my system was so frail that the doses I was able to take had no noticeable impact.

As the months wore on, I could see that Scott was distancing himself from me. When he would come home from work he rarely came in to check on me. I knew Scott loved me deeply and he was also dealing with his own health challenges. Still recovering from a bout of pancreatitis from the previous year, he would come home exhausted after long days of assisting his clients at work, and he needed to focus on his own health. While I recognized this, I also felt that when I needed him most was when he was furthest away from me. I felt betrayed by God, my spiritual guides, my husband, and my body. I was angry and felt incredibly hopeless.

In search of more information, I contacted two friends that are both master astrologers for readings of my astrological chart. One focused on Western astrology while the other focused on Eastern astrology. Both readings indicated past lives that were influencing me and my health, and that I was in a fight for my life that would take several years for me to fully heal. They both confirmed that my health was affected in my digestion and my nerves and that one day I would gain a greater understanding of my life purpose. I had already struggled for what seemed like an eternity and to hear that there were years more of this scared me, but I was grateful for the confirmation from the stars that there was more going on than I realized.

At this point, I needed to shift more of my attention from "How did this happen?" to "What can I do to heal that will help others that are also struggling?" I recognized that I was still in a great deal of fear and that most of my internal dialog was focused on "Why Me?" I was dedicated to moving forward and to doing the work necessary to be free of emotional and physical pain. I needed to find purpose for the challenges I was experiencing. It became important for me to stop identifying as the victim of circumstance and recognize that the challenges I had were there for me to learn from, and that if I had these challenges, others may have them as well. And thus, I share with you what I have learned along the way.

CHAPTER 4

It's All Connected

I now know the journey to wellness is not limited to what I once believed to be the three foundations of health: quality food, adequate sleep, and some form of exercise a few days a week. This was the prescription for nearly all ailments of yesterday. Although these are still fundamental elements for a healthy physical constitution, they don't fulfill our deep need for mental and emotional healing.

The stressors that our ancestors experienced were often singular incidents that momentarily caused a spike in adrenaline and the release of cortisol into the body. Today, we have a constant bombardment of stressors flying at us. It's become a status symbol to get less sleep and use energy drinks or supplements to bypass the signals of the body to slow down. Instead, we often push harder rather than get the needed rest. We are no longer limited to our corner of the world with family, friends, work relationships, and church responsibility all vying for our attention. We're often hit with the world's problems the moment we pick up our phones or turn on the television. Friends may be posting pictures of the amazing time they had the night before where we weren't invited and a heavy dose of FOMO and jealousy rushes through us.

We exist in a world of instant gratification. We want faster internet, instant access to movies and music, and our meals to be quick and easy. Fast food restaurants now have multiple lanes in the drive-through to accommodate the demand. Popular social media posts are geared for "hacking" tasks toward greater efficiency and speed. There are never enough hours in the day to accomplish the laundry list of demands on our time, depleting our energy and causing a huge amount of stress and physical breakdown. Our children are over-scheduled and incoming texts chime throughout the day.

It is not socially acceptable to allow ourselves to take time to heal. Many of us are conditioned to believe that if we are not in the mode of accomplishment then we are letting our lives waste away. You may not always recognize the direct impact of stress or illness in your life, as it is common to adapt and develop a "new normal." Often this happens so gradually that it takes a concrete inventory to gain a clear perspective from where you may have been to the conditions of your current health. Awareness can happen by coming across a photo of yourself when you were physically toned and your body looked strong and full of vitality, or coming across an old journal entry where you felt excitement for an upcoming 10 k run.

Illness often slithers in so gradually that it is almost unrecognizable until the "big one" hits. It's only in your 20/20 hindsight that signals are blaring the alert. These signals can show up in a variety of ways. You may begin limiting engaging with others after work because you feel worn out or you restrict activities that you used to thrive in because your recovery period takes longer now. Slowly, over time, you make your life smaller. This can also happen when someone experiences emotional trauma and closes out loved ones as an act of self-preservation. We think we are protecting ourselves from feelings of anxiety or fear but by closing ourselves off we limit the support that was once available to us.

Many illnesses that arrive slowly or are easy to miss at the onset are labeled as "autoimmune diseases." In essence, these are considered diseases where the immune system attacks healthy tissue. I had multiple symptoms that fell in the categories of Crohn's disease, fibromyalgia, chronic fatigue, and celiac disease, which are each labeled as an autoimmune disease.

Medically speaking, there are now over eighty autoimmune diseases, many of which overlap in classic symptoms of chronic fatigue, digestive issues, pain and inflammation, flu-like symptoms, and low-grade fever. Diagnosis of autoimmune diseases has tripled within the last fifty years.

Unfortunately, we are just barely on the cusp of understanding the body's relationship with our immune system. I adamantly believe that an immune response such as this is the body's warning signal indicating deeper issues that need to be addressed—not what is claimed in the medical community, that the body is attacking itself. The wisdom of the human body exceeds our capacity to measure and understand—far more than we realize. Even with multiple symptoms and health providers attempting to label my illness as an autoimmune condition, I knew that my body was never attacking itself. To believe that you are under attack from your own body is the most dangerous thought you can have. Your body is NEVER attacking itself. If you get nothing more from this book I pray that you understand this. Under the right circumstances, your body is designed to self-regulate and heal. Trust that you are receiving guidance via physical symptoms to make adjustments. Understand that your body and mind are in constant communication. And you, a soul inhabiting this body, may not have the awareness of what this communication is. Symptoms are your body's form of communication that something is out of balance, giving you the awareness to adjust various areas of your life, such as your diet, emotions, thoughts, or your environment.

Because of this deep connection, it's important to let go of everything that is not supportive to your emotional and physical well-being. This may sound drastic but illness sucks; if you want to heal, you likely need to let some things go, including toxic relationships. I have always felt that some people come into our lives to remind us of what we don't want in life. By recognizing certain characteristics that you do not want in your life, you get more clarity on what you *do* want to attract.

You may have heard the statement "It's not the destination but the journey that counts." However, when you are neck deep in physical pain and fear for your life, the last thing you want to hear are fluffy words of inspiration. Pain and fear are not an inspiring space to be in. This is why, when others assume they are being supportive by offering words of encouragement, you may have a sense that you're not understood and ultimately, unsafe around others. Like me, you may think, "I could care less about the journey—just get me to the destination and make it fast." This response is rooted in the emotions of fear. It is human nature to want to dash through the challenges and desire for time to stand still in moments of joy and bliss. We experience life on the emotional, physical and mental levels of our being and our healing is tied to each of these as well.

Everything truly is connected. In the following chapters I share with you the adjustments that can give greater support to your healing experience and the tools necessary to make those adjustments.

CHAPTER 5

Beliefs and Mindset

When you enter the depths of an illness, one of the mechanisms that eventually kicks in is self-reflection. Your brain is wired to search for answers under stress and you are forced to confront your beliefs. Your mind begins playing back every experience from your past, over and over, looking for that one thing that you possibly missed. You ask yourself repeatedly, "How could this be happening to ME?" Suddenly, you are caught up in a whirlwind of emotions and feel a sense of internal ground zero, when all bets are off and everything that you thought or believed is up for cross-examination.

At first, nothing makes sense in your outer world. You feel angry and unsafe because some force out there didn't protect you. You have been thrust from security into the harshness of a new reality. Your mind continues to search for answers and look for ways to keep you safe. Realizing that you can't find those answers in your outer world, you are forced to look within and reflect on what you know and believe.

Nobody attended a high school class where the teacher stood at the front of the room addressing crisis in health. You didn't have a textbook explaining what happens when your world implodes due to illness. There wasn't a reference guide handed to you as you entered adulthood, outlining specific emotional disturbances that you would experience, such as anger, grief, fear, or betrayal. You were not handed a list of resources and healing techniques that could help you if your life unwinds. And yet, life threw you a curveball and you are now in a battle with the only body that you have, hoping that the tools and resources you need to survive will be within reach. You may find yourself on an emotional roller coaster of hope and despair, moving from "I can overcome this" to "what's the use in trying—my life isn't worth living anyway" all in the same day.

Often with illness, there isn't anyone in your inner circle of friends or family that has experienced what you are now going through. Leaving them, and you, with little or no understanding of what you are truly experiencing. You begin looking around your environment and wonder why everyone else is behaving as if life is "normal" when nothing is normal in your life anymore. You may feel that society has officially failed you, that life isn't fair, and that you don't deserve to go through this illness. You may begin questioning yourself on what you did wrong.

It is important to catch yourself when negative emotions come up and consciously choose to keep your attention on what is good in your life. We see what we choose to see. By focusing on what is good you can align yourself with hope and gratitude. I respect the challenges in coming up with something to be grateful for when your life is unraveling, especially when you are in physical pain and nothing about your body seems to be going right. If it feels too challenging to start with feelings of gratitude for your life and your body, start by feeling gratitude for past experiences that brought you great joy. By recalling a joyful experience, you align your emotions with joy and are more likely to feel gratitude where you are today.

Your thoughts and beliefs matter. Before I go into detail about beliefs, allow me to share with you some relevant background about how you acquire beliefs in the first place. I will begin with a brief overview of how our brains work and will go into greater detail later in this chapter.

From the moment of conception your brain began developing your personality and temperament. A child's brain functions predominantly below creative consciousness in the theta brain wave state during the first seven years of life, recording vast amounts of information needed for survival in their environment. According to Dr. Bruce Lipton, children do not express the quality of consciousness associated with alpha, beta, and gamma wave activity, the activity that governs much of the conscious daily thinking of an adult, as a predominant brain state. This limits their mental capacity to consciously evaluate whether the information they are receiving is beneficial or detrimental to their life. The information recorded in the subconscious mind during the first seven years continues to shape your subconscious behavior and sets the tone for continued behavior patterns into adulthood.

Your subconscious mind is profoundly more influential in your behavior than your conscious mind; with over forty million nerve impulses per second, it is one million times more powerful than the conscious mind. To understand how the brain shapes our behavior and beliefs, we should take a deeper look at the various brain wave frequencies at play. There are five different brain wave frequencies: delta (the lowest frequency), theta, alpha, beta, and gamma (the highest frequency). Each frequency is measured in cycles per second (Hz) and has specific characteristics needed for the different levels of brain activity and consciousness. All humans display these five brain wave frequencies or electrical patterns across the cortex; however, one particular brain wave will be dominant depending on the state of consciousness. Each frequency has a different purpose for mental functioning in relation to our various day-to-day life experiences—supporting everything from active learning of new information to deep sleep.

There are various activity levels that correspond to the different brain wave states, each valuable in meeting various needs. To improve your ability to visualize and create your ideal life you may need to spend additional time each day in activities that will drop your brain waves into the lower frequencies of delta, alpha, and theta, which support healing and nervous system regeneration (two excellent activities with this effect are tapping and meditation, techniques that will be covered in greater detail in chapter 8). In turn, this decreases the time you spend in beta and gamma states, which are more active and stimulating but are not productive for healing and regeneration of the body.

Having an awareness of how your brain responds to different

environments and levels of activity will give you an understanding of the adjustments that you may need to make in your lifestyle patterns to optimize your healing potential. To help you gain a greater appreciation for how your brain works, I will briefly describe the different types of brain wave frequencies, their purposes, when we experience them, and how they affect us.

Delta waves, the slowest recorded brain waves in human beings, have a frequency range of 0 Hz to 4 Hz. This is the dominant frequency in infants and young children. As we age, we tend to produce less delta wave activity even during deep sleep; this frequency remains essential to our health, though, no matter what our age. Healing and regeneration are enhanced in this state, making delta waves essential to the healing process. These waves are involved in unconscious bodily functions such as regulating heartbeat and digestion and are generated in the deepest levels of sleep, relaxation, and meditation.

Theta waves have a frequency range of 4 Hz to 8 Hz. This frequency is involved in daydreaming, relaxation, and restorative sleep and is the state of creation. Theta's imaginative state helps us to envision the life that we want to create, helping enhance our intuition and creativity. Theta waves are connected to the experience of feeling deep emotions. Due to the deeply relaxed state of consciousness they induce, the theta wave state is highly suggestible and useful in hypnotherapy or past life regression. This is a dreamy state of consciousness where it is common to see images appear in your mind's eye, where you are on the cusp of falling to sleep and begin to see dream images before actual sleep. The theta state is attainable during a guided imagery exercise or a meditation where you begin to feel a sense of heaviness in your body as it relaxes into a deeper state.

Alpha waves have a frequency range of 8 Hz to 12 Hz. These waves are the bridges between our conscious mind and subconscious mind. They help us calm down when necessary and promote feelings of deep relaxation. Frequencies in the midrange of alpha (as well as theta) are optimal for experiencing your creative power through visualization and using your imagination. To achieve the alpha state, practice deep rhythmic breathing to relax your body. Releasing tension and worry from your mind will drop you down into the alpha brain state.

Beta waves have a frequency range of 12 Hz to 30 Hz. Beta activity is involved in conscious thought. This frequency is most common in children from between eight to twelve years of age and adults who are awake and active. Most people exhibit beta waves throughout the day to complete conscious tasks such as critical thinking, writing, reading, and socialization. Since you are naturally in the beta state when you are fully awake, this state takes very little effort to obtain and maintain.

Gamma waves have a frequency range from 40 Hz to 100 Hz. This frequency range is involved in higher processing tasks as well as cognitive functioning, and is important for learning, memory, and information processing. Gamma waves are associated with expanded awareness and heightened intuition and are highest among people that meditate regularly. Accessing the gamma frequency is achieved through acts of compassion and through love of self and others.

All of these brain waves influence our beliefs. In simple terms, a belief is a thought that you continue to think, either consciously or subconsciously. These thoughts are accepted and considered to be true by you. Your beliefs act as the filtering system of your every experience and so affect every aspect of your life, shaping your relationship with religion, politics, presumed social status, financial security, other people, self-value, and your HEALTH.

From the very beginning of your existence you began to form beliefs that settled into your subconscious as truth by your interpretation of experiences. Your beliefs and values were predominantly determined and influenced by your culture, parents, friends, religious leaders, and media and political figures, as well as your assumptions and misunderstandings in your environment. Through your personal views of the world, beliefs are formed via experiences that reinforced your previous perceptions. Your beliefs are personal and can change based upon new knowledge and understanding resulting from a shift in awareness where you view your life from a larger perspective rather than your ego self.

Once you have a belief, any incoming information is filtered through your subconscious; information that aligns with your original belief is generally accepted and strengthens your conviction and any information that contradicts your belief is generally rejected. Whether or not the incoming information or experience is factual to anyone else. You will shape your perceptions and judgements to support what you feel is true in that moment. Knowing that every aspect of your life is influenced by your beliefs, the next questions you need to ask yourself is, "What if my beliefs are wrong? And if they are, how do I change them?"

Changing your beliefs is a matter of choosing to be conscious of the thoughts that you are having, questioning the thoughts and beliefs that are no longer relevant or beneficial toward your healing, and choosing to form a new belief. This new belief is now added to your list of truths. A simple way to create your new truth is to state it repeatedly, preferably out loud, in the form of an affirmation or declaration. Your mind will begin looking for evidence that this truth is a fit and by your repeated statements declaring it is so, your attention will be drawn toward external evidence that is confirming. Eventually, your subconscious mind accepts this as a new truth. For me, I was very clear that there wasn't a single belief that I had created or that had been downloaded into my subconscious that held more value than healing and being free of physical pain. Getting clear about your beliefs and making a conscious decision to adjust or remove beliefs that no longer serve you will be paramount in attracting the vibration of healing.

Pay attention to when your mind tries to revert into a familiar behavior or pattern and remember that your mind is simply doing what it was made to do—keep you safe with what you know. Be open to expanding your consciousness and look for possibilities for growth in awareness.

My first introduction to addressing beliefs associated with illness was through the pioneering work in medical intuition and energy healing of Caroline Myss. Myss's understanding of the healing experience is enormous and her ability to track the energy of illness back to its origin was groundbreaking. Caroline Myss was the first to coin the term "medical intuitive" when she began working with neurosurgeon Dr.

Norm Shealy. Shealy tested Myss's intuitive abilities to see illness in other people, even before that person was aware of the illness, with an accuracy level of 93 percent, which is the highest accuracy rate documented.

When I heard Myss lecture about getting real with the beliefs that we have and how they affect our life, it became brutally evident to me that to heal I had to break down every belief that I believed to be true down to the core level of my subconscious. According to Myss, our beliefs can either serve us or handicap us. The problem is that most people don't even know what they believe until they are forced to look directly at where they stand on an issue, and this isn't usually addressed until their beliefs are threatened in some way. But, I was willing to do the work necessary to heal. I journeyed deep into my consciousness through meditation, prayer, journaling, conscious awareness of my inner dialog, and choosing to limit my connection to outside distractions so that I could be an active listener to beliefs that would surface from within. I also paid keen attention to my body language in response to my outside environment. I understood the relationship of mind and body in which the brain is acting as the conscious mind and the body as the subconscious mind. When the different thoughts and beliefs showed up I made note to look deep into my root beliefs and categorize these beliefs into two separate categories, "My Truth" and "Universal Truth."

I would categorize a belief as My Truth if it only applied to me and/or my environment or demographic and categorized other beliefs as a Universal Truth if it applied to the whole of humanity. Universal Truths never change. Their scope is not limited by race, country of origin, religion, social or financial status, gender, generation, or good deeds.

It can often be difficult to discern what is in fact a Universal Truth. You may, for example, believe that your religious teachings or upbringing are a Universal Truth because, in your perception, these are truths that do apply to everyone—if only "everyone" would get on board with what you believe to be true. Yet, more often than not, the differences in religious teachings come down to a simple example of personal beliefs—in other words, varying individual truths. When you find a truth that applies to all religions and spiritual teachings, you will see that it is a Universal Truth and one to pay attention to.

I would like to make clear, I am not suggesting that all your personal beliefs or truths need to change. Most of who you are is based on what you hold true and it would take a lifetime to extrapolate what you believe in every circumstance. However, most of us have lived many years unaware of what we identify with. Having the willingness to examine beliefs allows you to determine whether they are still a good fit for you or not.

When we thoughtfully examine our beliefs, we often discover how few of them are based in Universal Truth. I encourage you to not view yourself from a perspective of having been wrong, but rather appreciate that you are willing to expand your awareness. In looking at my list of personal beliefs, I discovered that they were limited in perception, and if I chose to stay in this level of thinking, I was potentially holding myself back from truly healing. I chose to take a raw look at myself to find the Universal Truth, and to eliminate everything that was hindering my progression toward health.

In your own discovery, I encourage you to keep in mind that many beliefs were formed when you were a young child. Be as gentle with yourself as you would with a child that is learning a new skill such as walking. You wouldn't condemn and hurt a child for missteps in this phase of development but rather celebrate and feel joy in their advancement as they begin to move forward.

As noted earlier, recognize that as an adult, many of the beliefs you have are not even yours in the first place, but rather beliefs held by the adults around you, downloaded into your subconscious mind when you were a child via overheard conversation or seen behaviors. A conditioned belief that is negative or disempowering may have been seated in your subconscious for many years. You then strengthened this belief over time based upon the evidence provided in your environment. Seeing an old belief that is no longer serving you is not an opportunity to criticize yourself; it's an opportunity for growth.

Please note that having the awareness of the thoughts that you are having is one thing, changing these thoughts is a whole other ball game. Although it is very simple to change your thoughts, it is not easy. It takes consistency and dedication to root out beliefs that you have held your entire life. Many of these thoughts were originally created to keep your life safe and familiar, and because your beliefs were formed around the people that you held dear in your primary years, to go against these thoughts and perceptions can cause you to feel threatened in the security of your primary relationships.

I recommend that you keep a journal during your exploration, writing down thoughts that are coming up as well as the emotions that you are feeling. Not only is this a great reference showing how far you have come but the act of writing down what thoughts you are having will assist the energy to move through you and onto paper, where you will have more control of these thoughts rather than letting them slip in and out of your mind at random.

This can be an emotional experience—you may fear that your foundation in life will suddenly crumble and your life will fall apart. Let me put this fear to rest. A shift in your belief will always benefit you and those around you when this shift is to a higher vibration than the one that you had before. This opens the door for your healing and hopefully will assist you in letting go of the painful emotions of your past and support feeling gratitude for the blessings in your life.

While a shift to a higher vibration will ultimately benefit those around you, I recommend that you initially not share with others that you are about to change your beliefs and shift into new perceptions. This can feel threatening to loved ones who will immediately wonder how your new perceptions will affect them. I suggest that you spend time in self-reflection, making note of your internal dialog in response to how others behave around you in relation to your expectations of them. By having this expanded awareness you can utilize your time spent with others to help drive this reflection. After all, there is no greater opportunity to have your beliefs smack you in the face than when you are with family that share the same beliefs. I assure you, they will come up in conversation when you are ready to listen. Watch for comments made at family gatherings. (Remember those cringe-worthy holidays when your Aunt Martha thought out loud her opinion about your sister's new boyfriend she met at college?) Other great opportunities for self-evaluation are when you are watching movie genres you wouldn't normally gravitate toward or, when a family life event comes up such as a wedding or birth of a child. If you want to zero in on this fast, look up high school classmates on Facebook. Notice your immediate judgement of those who have struggled with weight, got divorced, or went to rehab. Also be aware of your thoughts of comparison to those who have traveled the world, got that dream job, or ended up with the hot husband. Stay conscious of what thoughts and emotions bubble to the surface. The key here is to ask yourself which beliefs about others could be limiting yourself and to recognize that change can happen. When you are aware of your own inner criticism or judgement you can expand these judgements to see if they apply as a whole. If not, it may be time to let some of that baggage go. Continue to stay aware by being the observer of your subtle thoughts when you have any health setback or are beginning any new healing treatments. Beliefs specifically related to your own health are the most important beliefs to uncover.

Once you have zeroed in on a specific belief that you want to change, you will need to create a new belief to override it. The simplest way to do this is to take a piece of paper and create two columns. In the first column, write down as specifically as possible exactly what your belief is currently. It's always valuable to see where your beliefs are to get more understanding of where you want to go. In the second column, choose a statement that contradicts the original belief and magnifies the qualities of this upgraded statement with additional positive words to describe the new mindset or behavior that you want to adopt. This new identifying statement is called a declaration or affirmation. (For consistency, I will refer to these statements as declarations.)

Begin by writing down a sentence or two specifically stating your new beliefs as if they already exist. Word your declarations in first person, beginning with "**I am**" as a way of identifying this belief with yourself to your brain. Keep these statements simple and easy to memorize.

Every time you speak, you are creating and confirming a vibrational frequency. Unfortunately, people are often unconscious about the words they are using and most of the statements we say tend to be negative. Whatever we identify as "**I am**" is instantly moving into alignment with us as a vibrational frequency so use these words with intention. Once you have your declarations written down, you will need to say them over and over until your mind recognizes your statements as truth. Repetition is the key to integrating any information into the subconscious. Repeat, repeat, repeat—until the beliefs are your new truth. Your brain will initially try to throw these statements out by reminding you that they aren't true. Take control and remind yourself that you can change. To reinforce any belief, you will continue to look for outside evidence whether it is true to anyone else or not. Deliberately look for and make note of outside evidence that reinforces your new truth. It's there; you just have to look for it. When you see this evidence, write it down and acknowledge it often to remind yourself of this truth.

Each of us vary in our ability to integrate a new belief. If your mind feels especially resistant, stay consistent and try not to allow your mind to drift back into past stories. If your mind does start to relive a past story or belief—and it will—catch it and proclaim, "Stop!" Then redirect your focus to your new truth by repeating your chosen declaration.

You may be thinking, "How can I say something that isn't true?" Remember that you have spent your entire life believing thoughts that came from someone else. In a world of illness, wouldn't it be amazing to have a level of control back in your hands by using words to empower you? Rewiring your brain by making conscious and deliberate declarations creates a new vibration that moves you toward wholeness and better health.

When you verbally declare your desires and ambitions, you are instantly sending out an energy of creation that will be matched in the physical form and become your new reality. Carefully chosen words that are positive and supportive to your healing process will eventually push out and replace old beliefs and purify your thoughts. By increasing the potency of the positive declaration, you will magnify your desired goal in the positive direction.

Commit to saying your declarations multiple times a day, changing the speed and volume to shift your brain into paying attention. Let go of any fear that if you take on a new belief, it will be forever tattooed into your subconscious, never allowed to leave again. Your perceptions will continue to shift, your awareness will continue to heighten, and you will go through more life experiences that will let you know when another shift needs to take place. Humanity is shifting on a global scale but not at the level and speed of what a person can do individually when you make the decision to be aware and create consciously.

One truth that I still believe is that illness doesn't just randomly happen and being whole and healed doesn't just happen either. I wasn't part of a lottery pool designed by an outside source and "gifted" the experience of illness. My illness was created by a variety of circumstances, including physical susceptibility, unhealed emotional traumas, and a limited mindset that kept me in the vibrational frequency of the experience.

Listed below are some of the beliefs that I had to uncover and redirect for my own healing. You may notice that many of my old beliefs involved blaming others or myself. These beliefs were disempowering and kept me in the victim role rather than being accountable for my own healing. I am sharing these beliefs to serve as a guidepost in your own discovery. At first glance you may resist thinking that any of these are also your beliefs. I resisted it too. Take an honest inventory of whether any of these apply to you as well.

You will notice that for every **Old Belief** listed below, I've included my **New Understanding** and suggested **Declaration** that I used to support forming a new belief. When you read some of my beliefs you may have an emotional response of criticism or judgement. Be gentle with yourself and listen to your inner guidance. Knowing that a great deal of these beliefs are common, I invite you to open your heart and mind as you journey with me through them. Rooting out old beliefs and replacing them with new ones is an opportunity for healing and expanding your consciousness. Allow yourself to uncover what is hidden below the surface.

My chosen declarations are designed to increase positive internal language and to potentize higher vibrational thoughts. If you recognize any of my old beliefs as ones currently holding you back, feel free to adjust the new declarations to meet your own needs and make it specific to you. Whether using the below declarations or others, I encourage you to initially say your new declarations with conviction, while standing erect with both feet firmly positioned on the ground. Keep a list of your declarations in a visible area to remind you to use them. I recommend that you keep a copy on your phone, on your bathroom mirror, on your refrigerator, or anywhere else that will trigger a reminder to continue to say them until they become your new truth. I always place a list of my declarations on the shower wall away from water flow and say them while I am in the shower.

Old Belief: If the people in my life would make changes in their behavior then I could finally make the changes that I need to make, so that I can finally heal.

New Understanding: This belief is much more common than you might expect. When you lack self-confidence, a common default is to blame others for your behavior. Yet no one is responsible for the actions that you take except you. Blaming others for not taking action on their behavior is an excuse to not make the changes that you know you need to make.

Declaration: "I make positive decisions each day that improve the quality of my health and body. I am accountable for my health and well-being."

Old Belief: Living is more painful than dying.

New Understanding: If you believe that your life is too painful to live you are subconsciously programming your body to break down and die. This belief may feel true temporarily but is a limited viewpoint that doesn't take into account that you have purpose on this planet. This viewpoint is self-defeating and stops the progression of healing.

Declaration: "I have a vibrant life full of joy and fun. I have a great purpose for living and I add value to other people's lives."

Old Belief: Other people's lifestyle and behaviors should cause them to be sick rather than me. It's not fair that I am sick and they are not.

New Understanding: This thinking is very limited and based upon what we see in a specific moment in time, which is never the full story. Judging behavior that someone else is doing, such as eating from the drive-through, smoking, or living a sedentary lifestyle, and then determining that these behaviors equal illness and disease will set you up for an emotional storm. By holding your attention on others, you are giving yourself permission to not do your own work. Comparing yourself to others always leads to judgment of two people—the other person and yourself. I was surprised by how many times I measured my health by observing other people. I realized that it wasn't my role to decide another person's destiny. I don't have power over what led them to where they are but I do have power in how I treat myself and others. By allowing each person to choose their life for themselves, I could keep my attention on healing rather than feeling like a victim.

Declaration: "I allow others to live their life fully and I engage with my own needs to heal and care for myself. I am responsible for my own healing."

Old Belief: Others should feel obligated to take care of my needs because that's what I would do for them if they were sick.

New Understanding: Again, this prompted me to compare myself with others and caused me to feel resentment. My perceptions of how others should behave was fueled by emotion rather than truth. It is obviously a moral decision to care for someone that is in a weakened or vulnerable state but to believe that others are obligated is non-sustaining and sets you up for unfulfilled expectations.

Declaration: "I have a great support system in my life. My needs are always met and others want the best for me."

Old Belief: I must stay productive. If someone sees me in bed resting during the day they will think that I am lazy.

New Understanding: This belief is rooted in stories from the past and has no value in healing. One of the biggest challenges for someone that is in a healing crisis is to integrate self-care, and many healers will pinpoint the lack of self-care as one of the key breakdowns of the body. Resting is valuable in the healing process. Expectations that you need to be productive are self-imposed. Creativity and inspiration occur in a rested and peaceful state; therefore, you are increasing your ability to heal by taking the time to rest when you need to.

Declaration: "I honor my body's needs and listen to my inner guidance. I take great care of my body and treat myself with love and respect. I give my body the rest that it needs to heal properly."

Old Belief: If I do everything right, such as eat well and get proper rest and exercise, my body will stay healthy.

New Understanding: Proper nutrition and exercise are significant factors in better health and vibrancy, but disease has multiple layers of causation. Viruses, fungi, parasites, environmental toxins, and genetically modified organisms can all negatively influence your health. Layering this with negative emotions and stress can wreak havoc on your well-being. For me, the undercurrent of this belief was that if I was a good girl, it meant that God's blessings were at my disposal. Being "good" gave me a sense that I would be placed at the front of the line to benefit from God's healing abilities. Believing that God was responsible for my illness and my healing was based on a false cycle of reward and punishment. God does not punish. My life, like all others, follows the laws of nature, which seek balance.

Declaration: "My body has the ability to heal. I provide all that my body needs to heal and stay healthy. God's grace is available to me and I am loved exactly how I am. I am healed and in perfect balance."

Belief: I need to know how much longer this illness will last in order for me to endure what I am going through.

New Understanding: This was one of my most challenging beliefs to surrender. A need to know why and how much longer you will go through an experience is a survival mechanism that's natural to everyone. We feel that if we have a sense of how long we will need to suffer, we can, for a time, shift into a mode of endurance fueled by brute force. The problem with this is that time is subjective. There is no way that a magic ball can answer this question because there are too many variables in healing. This thinking keeps you focused on the problem rather than allowing space for the solution to appear. By releasing the need to know and trusting in divine timing, you allow for your healing to take place more effortlessly.

Declaration: "I trust in divine timing and allow the necessary time for healing to take place for my highest good."

Old Belief: The answers to my healing are outside of me. If I talk to enough people or read enough books then someone will have the secret to my healing.

New Understanding: Every person needs to know that their healing comes from within and not from an external source. There may have been multiple components that contributed to disease and illness but you must trust that healing is within you. Be mindful that you may not be aware of all the forces of nature that are working for you.

Declaration: "I have all that I've ever needed for my body to heal. I realign in perfect harmony with God's truth. My body is healthy, strong, vibrant, and whole."

Old Belief: I need to focus on illness as the problem that needs to be fixed.

New Understanding: My focused attention on what was out of balance only enhanced the energy of what I didn't want. Continued thoughts and attention on the problem of illness only serve to magnify it. By shifting your attention to wellness, you open the door for possibilities of healing and being whole.

Declaration: "I love my body and I am grateful for all that it gives me. I am healed."

Old Belief: In my continued suffering I am burning off karma. I must deserve illness for God will only give to us what we deserve.

New Understanding: If you believe in the laws of karma then this may be a tough one to let go of. Karma is not a punisher but rather a balancer of nature. We did not enter life to suffer and to be held in bondage. This is much different than experiencing challenges which are necessary for growth. Each of us experience challenges but this does not need to equate to suffering. In releasing the belief that suffering is necessary, you allow the higher forces of nature to take place.

Declaration: "I trust in the laws of nature for my highest good. Divine healing energy is always available to me."

These declarations may be a starting point for you. But it's important to thoroughly look at your own life and beliefs to see where else you may be undermining your own healing.

When your thoughts project into your future, what images come up in how you see your life? Do you see lifelong suffering, multiple medications, chronic pain, and being housebound, or do you see yourself vibrant, healthy, and strong? Are you living and experiencing life as a fun adventure, participating in the activities that you enjoy?

Your future has not been created yet in the physical form but your beliefs and thoughts about your future are in creation every moment. For you to heal, you must believe that it is possible.

In activating any belief, negative or positive, there is an instantaneous cellular response within your body. This is essential, so I will say it again: for healing to occur, you must BELIEVE THAT YOU CAN AND WILL HEAL! Once you shift your mind, you've shifted into an intention. When you set an intention to heal, you have triggered the healing to begin within your body. On a conscious level most people desire to heal. (I say most because there are people that don't feel purpose or joy in life and believe that the way out of their suffering is to have illness and, eventually, death.) But this conscious desire isn't enough—your subconscious beliefs regarding healing must also be in alignment with your conscious mind in knowing that you will heal.

The following beliefs are important to integrate into your subconscious to allow healing to take place:

You must believe that you can and will heal. Remember that the human body is designed to heal itself under the right conditions.

You must believe that it is your right to heal and to live a life of vitality and abundance. We are not meant to suffer. We will experience challenges for growth but suffering is an emotional response to the conditions that you are experiencing, and experiencing challenges does not need to go hand in hand with suffering.

You must trust that your body is your ally and your friend. It is not attacking you (no matter what current medical beliefs are saying). Your body was created to serve you as a vehicle for growth. There isn't something sinister residing in the recesses of your DNA out to destroy you. But rather, your body is communicating to you that there is an imbalance that needs attention. This communication may show up as a tumor, inflammation, intestinal distress, physical pain, or a host of other concerns. Even as your body communicates to you through these means, you must view and trust your body as supporting your wellness.

You must believe that your mind, body, and spirit are intrinsically connected as a single system and that by shifting and improving one area, the other areas must change too.

You must believe that there is a higher force working for you and not against you in driving you closer to your purpose.

You must believe that the people in your life have the desire for you to be healthy and whole and will support you in making this decision.

If you can begin to accept these truths on the deepest level, you will be opening yourself up to the healing potential within you. As you do this, remain conscious of behaviors that are not in alignment with your healing. Once you have awareness of a behavior that you want to change, create a new declaration to support that change in behaviors. Be patient with yourself. Your mind and body don't always adjust at the same speed. When there is a desired mindset transformation, it can take some time for your body to catch up and adjust to your beliefs. Continue to be gentle with your body and declare your desired truths. Your world is yours to design.

CHAPTER 6

Elements of Creation

As a member of the human race, you are a co-creator of your life path. You are neither a simple pawn on the world stage playing out the wishes and demands of some outer force of evil or good and you are not the sole executor of your life experience. First of all, there is none among us that is capable of wielding that type of power. Just imagine the many thoughts you have had in your life that, thankfully, did not come into fruition. We live in a world of emotions and struggle where each of us have engaged in thoughts that were not kind either to ourselves or others. We also do not have the consciousness in this third-dimension reality to fully understand the impact our desires could have on others or ourselves. We are impulsive and lack the clarity of mind needed to truly hold the command of ultimate creator. We are, however, key players in our life experience.

You are an energetic being of light that is connected to all of life consciousness, co-creating all that is around you with the universal energy that is God. Before you entered this life, your soul contributed to specific decisions in the creation of your life experience. You chose which parents, siblings, and children you would have. You decided on which areas your soul wanted to focus attention on for personal growth and what karmic debts you would work out, which limitations you would struggle with, which gifts you came to enhance, relationships you would encounter, and specific opportunities for spiritual growth.

You entered life with a supportive energy to guide you toward experiences and encounters that would allow for opportunities to heal experiences from past incarnations and to gain wisdom as a spiritual being for your soul's progression. Gaining a clear understanding of this fundamental law will give you the clarity to put yourself back in the driver seat in your healing journey.

I want to be clear that it doesn't matter what religious background you have or what name you call the force of energy that is greater than all things. Healing and co-creating are not about religion; they are about bringing the mind, body, and spirit back into alignment.

The specific elements of creation are your thoughts, words, vision, and emotions, with the two most powerful being your thoughts and your emotions. Your thoughts are the communication from your brain and your emotions are the communication from your body.

Your brain is both conscious and subconscious. Your conscious mind is in the prefrontal cortex and manages what you desire in life. The conscious mind is creative in its ability to visualize the past and the future and jumps from thought to thought, answers questions, and makes decisions. The subconscious mind is a database of stored programs, primarily derived from the programming a child receives as early as the last trimester in utero. Yes—the subconscious mind starts responding in utero, before birth. Any repeated pattern by the mother is learned by the fetus and programmed into the subconscious mind. This is where beliefs come in. Your subconscious behaviors are not thought-out responses but rather conditioned responses derived from your environment, via your parents, siblings, and community. And many of them are negative. This isn't to say that the people around you were innately negative—after all, most parents truly want the best for their children and desire to keep them safe—but the messages they sent out, often unintentionally, often were. Psychology reveals up to 70 percent of these "learned" behaviors are disempowering, self-sabotaging, and limiting.

These programmed behaviors are expressed as energetic vibrations that are not contained within your head but are broadcast out into your environment. Your brain sends out these vibrations based upon the thoughts that you have, consciously and subconsciously. You also receive vibrations from your environment that reinforce the beliefs that are already rooted deep within your subconscious. Changing old patterns has the potential to be the most powerful discipline of your life, yet unless you have specific guidelines and tools for transformation, you will soon reverse back to where you are currently.

To change these programed behaviors, it's important to be clear about where you are now and where you want to be in regards to your personal life and your health. To do so, begin by describing how you view yourself. Most people define who they are by the roles that they have in other people's lives and by their past experiences. But I'd like you to remember that you are more than these things.

Take a few moments and write a one-page description, from your point of you, about who you are. You may feel challenged to write anything more than a few sentences but push yourself to do it. Subconscious beliefs are rooted deep within and it takes conscious effort to reveal how you truly see yourself. Your brain will have to search for information to complete a full page.

You will receive the greatest benefit by being honest with yourself. Don't edit what comes to mind for fear that you will be judged by your answers. This is strictly for your eyes only. If a thought comes to mind as you write, it is layered somewhere in your subconscious. Go ahead now. I will wait…

In reviewing your description of how you see yourself, you have the opportunity to make adjustments in areas where you may not be living to your highest good. This description of yourself is a starting point of reference but not your rule manual. Recognize things that may not be true but you tell yourself anyway. Look for ways that you may be carrying a belief that no longer fits. Date your paper and tuck it away in your journal to later reflect on how you used to see yourself. Then take the reins in your healing and ask yourself the following questions:

Do I allow myself to get caught up in a cycle of self-deprecating internal dialogue?

- Do I keep painful memories of my past active in conversations with others?

- Do I look in the mirror with disgust, resentment, and hate?

- Do others avoid me because when they ask how I am feeling, I respond with a half hour speech about the struggles I endure?

- Do I look for opportunities to share with others how hard my life is?

- Do I prepare a laundry list of complaints for my next doctor appointment?

- Do I sabotage my healing by not eating well or engaging in reckless behavior?

These are all areas to look at directly to see how you may be continuing the perpetuation of illness. To change your vibration from one that is struggling to one of health and vitality you must change on every level of consciousness. Make a commitment in writing down specific improvements that you want to incorporate. Detail the daily steps you will take toward these improvements and sign it. It may be helpful to share this with someone that will support your efforts and keep you accountable.

THOUGHTS

Soon after becoming sick you may have experienced thoughts of overwhelm and despair, feeling fear and hopelessness as to what the future holds for you. Not only is your mind trying to find answers from your past, but you fear the unknown world before you. To co-create your future in the direction you desire and make an improvement in your life, you must change the thoughts that you have, the language that you use, and the vision that you see for your life. Be conscious of every word that comes out of your mouth and catch yourself if your language goes into self-deprecation or focuses on illness, disease, and fear. I know what you are thinking as you're reading this: "But I am sick and I do hurt and I do feel fear, and besides, I am only saying what is true."

Many spiritual teachers will tell you that illness does not cause suffering but rather the thoughts that you have about your experience cause suffering. Your thoughts, language, and emotions are derived from your perception of yourself and your environment. By shifting your perception, even the slightest, you can shift the level of your health. Negative internal dialog is one of the biggest causes of lowering personal energy and only serves as a self-fulfilling prophecy, keeping you in a lowered energy state about yourself and wellness. For healing to take place you will need to stop feeding the negative thoughts and stories from your past.

If you are looking at your life from a limited perspective of illness and fear, then your ability to heal is limited as well. By shifting your thoughts from the pain, fear, illness, and disease, and placing your attention on possibility, vibrancy, and health, you co-create at the highest level. You accomplish this by using the powers of creation: your thoughts, words, vision, and emotions.

As a co-creator, you have the power to transform the circumstances of your life. When you are thinking about the circumstances that you're currently living, you are focused on the problem instead of the solution. By adjusting your thinking in search of solutions and adding the emotions of hope for the answers to come and gratitude for the healing you believe will take place, you have taken the first steps to becoming healed and whole.

There are few things in life that are more limiting and scary than chronic pain and illness. I know all too well how disempowering it feels to see other people enjoying their life—I even found myself feeling jealous of people being happy in TV commercials. This caused a cycle of self-judgment and my continually asking the same question. "Why me?" As long as I was focused on what was wrong, I was focused on the problem, and thus, co-creating an environment that kept me in the vibration of illness and pain.

Although you cannot control which thoughts enter your head, you can control how long those thoughts are allowed to stay. Do you allow your thoughts to focus on how your body is feeling right now? Do you feel yourself restricting and recoiling from the possibility of healing? Are you thinking in a limited manner? This may be happening through thoughts such as, "I have a terminal disease. My doctor said that I am going to die. My illness is untreatable. I'm too old to heal."

By adjusting your thoughts and asking empowering questions you open possibilities for the answers to arrive. When your mind feels peaceful, ask yourself the following questions:

- What do I need to change?
- What adjustments do I need to make in my behavior?
- How can I feel better?
- What relationships or behaviors do I have that are sabotaging my health?
- What healing modalities can I implement to improve my health?
- What do I need to release that is no longer bencfiting my life?

Then, listen for the subtle answers that appear naturally and begin implementing the changes that you need to make.

By having awareness, you can train your thoughts in the direction of where you desire to be and stop focusing on where you are. Be open to miracles and possibilities by focusing on the future of your life—the life that you are creating. You have always been a creator of your life. Now it is time to be a conscious creator by choosing thoughts that are empowering.

If it feels like it's too challenging for you to adjust your thoughts and perception, even slightly, look for opportunities to feel gratitude. Remember, thoughts are the signals from your brain and emotions are the signals from your body. They are in constant communication with one another. By entering the space of emotional gratitude your mind will let down its guard and find solutions to your healing. Feel grateful in this moment that you are still alive, awakening what is possible. Grateful that you have support in your healing. The feeling of gratitude shifts your perception and attention. Don't allow any negative thoughts to root themselves into your story of the life that you are creating. Believe that no matter where you are in your healing, your life in this body is going to transition into abundant health.

It takes skill and effort to train your mind. You will receive the greatest benefits by keeping your mind in present time rather than reliving and hashing out past experiences or focusing on an unknown future. In a state of awareness and being present in the here and now, we reclaim control of our thoughts, but if you are in a state of resistance and avoidance regarding what is going on in and around you, you will be pulled out of present time. Believe me, I spent years in so much physical pain that I became accustomed to doing anything that I could to avoid feeling and being in the present.

Make it a habit to choose awareness as one of your sidekicks. There are a few techniques that will support you in conditioning your mind to work for you rather than against you. These are meditation (I will go more into this in chapter 8), slow and deep breathing, gentle yoga exercises, journaling gratitude, spending time in nature, and staying consciously aware of when your old thought patterns show up.

As long as you are in the human form, you will not be perfect in your thought process. You are never going to be 100 percent in alignment with positive thoughts but when you have awareness of the power of your thoughts you will begin catching the negative ones quickly—at the gate—and transforming them instantly. To move your thoughts to the next level of creation, consciously connect to the source of all energy, God, within fifteen to twenty minutes of waking each morning. Sit in a comfortable position and direct your thoughts toward connecting with this healing energy. Quiet your mind and ask God/your spirit guides/your guardian angel the following question: "What can I learn from you today in regards to my health?" Just be still and trust that the answer will come. If you feel that your mind is just making things up or is too scattered to receive a valuable response, take a deep breath and calm your mind. Repeat the question and allow yourself to receive the answer. Believe that whatever enters your thoughts has purpose for you to consider.

Spirit is ALWAYS available to you and is always trying to communicate with you. It is resistance and lack of trust that prevents you from receiving the insight that you have been searching for. The messages are subtle and may show up as a visual image in your mind or a fleeting thought. You may have a sudden idea to reach out to a healer that someone recommended to you last week or to start integrating more live food into your diet, or an image of someone that you know may appear in your mind's eye as a person to connect with. Whatever you receive, trust it and write it down in a notebook. I know you think that you will remember it but trust me, if you don't write it down there is a high probability you will get distracted and forget, and the message will drift right back out of your awareness—another possible answer to your next level of healing, missed. Commit to yourself that you will take action on the message that you receive. Set a deadline that you will take that action within a reasonable time frame.

There exist untold vibrational levels on this planet. The lower vibrational frequencies are fear, guilt, hate, and anger. Whenever you allow your consciousness—which is your thoughts, feelings, and spoken words—to dwell on the lower vibrations you are allowing the quality of that vibration to be generated within and around you. Any thoughts below the vibration of love, joy, health, and vitality are created in the human level, but not by God.

WORDS

The words you use carry significant power. Sound is the movement and vibration of creation and it takes the spoken word to bring into manifestation what your heart desires. In reflection, you may recall how it only takes a few words in a conversation to either crush your heart or empower you into hope and excitement. To understand the impact that words carry, recall an experience in your past when a classmate, school teacher, sibling, or parent said something that still makes you cringe many years later. A single statement can have profound effects on decisions that you make throughout your entire life. Energetically, these experiences shrink our self-worth and cause us to engage in a smaller way.

Someone in the past may have said to you that you're not good for anything. Their intention and reference may have been in regards to a singular incident but your brain interpreted that to literally mean you are not good AT ANYTHING. The impact of this could limit you in pursuing a job opportunity, finding a new relationship, managing your finances, and healing your body.

Growing up is challenging for everyone. An off-the-cuff statement from a teacher that you admired or a cruel jab from one of your peers can significantly lower your self-value and limit you in untold ways. It's natural to internalize things that other people say to us and accept these statements as truth if we lack the confidence and self-value to assert our own truth. Unfortunately, we often give our power over to others in deciding what is true about us and what is not. The more someone struggles with self-value, the more likely they will resign themselves to other people deciding who they are and reinforcing these identifying aspects with the words they speak.

As noted earlier, the two most powerful and most used words in any language are "I am." When you use the words "I am" you immediately send a signal to every cell in your body and your environment of your intentions and desires. When you say any statement that contains the words "I am" you are setting in motion that expression to manifest. Because of this, it is of utmost importance to manage your language in claiming "I am" and only use these words in regards to what you truly desire.

It is common to think that you are just speaking what is true by saying I am in pain, or I am angry, or I don't feel well. Yet speaking in this manner identifies who you are by the sensations that your body is feeling. Your identity is not pain; you are an individual that is perceiving pain. To vocalize "I am" is to call forth more of what you perceive. Feeling pain, anger, or discomfort are expressed sensations in your body. You, as an individual, are processing these sensations—don't identify them as who you are instead of a feeling that you have.

Obviously, there are going to be times when someone will ask how you are doing. If this person is a health professional that needs to gauge your healing, you certainly can share whether you are improving or feel some decline to assist them on which direction to go in your healing protocol. But respond in brief statements rather than emotionally engaging stories. Clearly identify the specifics of what you are feeling but try not to anchor into the story that you have created along with the emotional and physical sensations. If you are feeling angry, unwell, or in pain you may need to say so, but rather than saying "I am in pain" or "I am angry," change the language to "right now I am feeling pain in this area of my body," or "right now I am feeling angry that my body is not responding appropriately." This subtle shift notifies your brain that these are temporary expressions that are moving through you rather than a desire of creation. Your brain does not know whether something is a perceived truth or an actual truth. By stating it as a feeling you are giving your brain permission to not signal your cells to activate more of what you don't want.

In the beginning, shifting your language can be challenging but if you continue to choose to be the master architect of your life, it will get easier. The more you declare something out loud and own your ability to create your life, the easier it will be to accept this as truth and to expect it to manifest into reality. Stop defending your challenges, symptoms, and discouragement, as a reminder to everyone around you that the burdens you carry are heavier than theirs. Illness and suffering is not a competition that anyone wants to win yet it is a very common competition that humanity engages in. It's amazing how often people try to "one up" one another by sharing their suffering as a badge of recognition or honor.

Nothing is more connecting on this planet than a shared past. It is a belief and validation that someone else understands who you are. Ask yourself if what you want is for someone else to know the depths of your sorrow, to pity you, and to feel sorry for you. Nobody truly wants others to pity them, but in telling the stories of your symptoms, fears, and journey through disease, that is what you are asking others to do. This stalls healing and is non-sustaining because people move on with their attention. Also, when sharing the depths of your challenges there can come a point where the conversation can go sideways. If you word vomit everything that you have gone through on someone else, you have no control how it is going to be received. If the other person doesn't have the ability or capacity to process what you said they can emotionally shut down and feel very uncomfortable, causing you to backpedal and go into a self-judgment.

Hold the belief that you will heal and use the words that are in alignment with such. Limit your attention on the symptoms that you are currently experiencing and expand your attention on what you desire by setting boundaries with yourself and others that the only dialogue you will allow in regards to your health is one of possibilities and hope.

Recognize that no matter how challenging your experiences have been there is never going to be a trophy at the end of this journey. You are not going to die and be received by a standing applause on the other side for your suffering. Believe in your heart that the only validation you need will come internally, when you are whole again.

VISION

You are not the center of *the* universe but rather the center of *your* universe. Meaning that everything that you see in your life is directly connected to the vibrations that you are putting out. When you see people that are vibrant and healthy, don't allow yourself to feel the emotions of resentment, anger, and exclusion. Adjust your thinking and see this as an opportunity and reminder to heal. Believe that you are seeing people that are healthy as a visual manifestation of what you internally desire.

The visual component that I am referring to is your internal vision, or your mind's eye, rather than the vision of your external environment. As a co-creator of your life and your health you need to be able to "see" yourself as healed. Take a moment and close your eyes. Visualize a mirror image of yourself standing before you. Get a clear image of the person standing in front of you and describe in detail who you see. If it is too challenging for you to visualize then you can write a one-page description of who you are. Include all the adjectives that come to mind and integrate your senses. Be creative. Describe in detail your facial expression, your clothing, your activity, the strength of your body, and the details in your environment that you would see in your mirror image. These are indicators of how you see yourself.

It is important to have a visual foundation when co-creating your life. Each person has their own version of what they see within. This is often a contributing factor to a communication gap, in relationships with others, between what one person says and what the other person hears. This is because every person filters all information through their visual understanding (as well as their beliefs).

Each of us base our internal vision on what we are familiar with. Take the word "bark" for instance. If you have a background where you spent time climbing trees as a child, or happen to work with lumber, you may instantly create a visual image of the rough edges and patterns in tree bark. But if you have a dog at home you may instantly see your dog and internally hear your dog's bark. Another example would be the word "nail." Did you visualize what is at the end of your fingers or a carpenter's tool? Now think of the word "pool." Did you immediately have an image of a game of billiards or the city swimming pool? Recognize how with each word an instantaneous image appeared in your mind's eye that was filtered through your history.

Now, take this concept to a deeper level. In these examples, did you notice that the word was not only the image that you saw, but rather a component of the whole? Again, using the word "pool," if you grew up with a backyard pool you may have seen not only an image of your swimming pool but an image of your backyard and multiple components of that image. Maybe the brick wall that separates your yard, or a tree, the grass, the color of the water, or someone jumping in. However, if in college you often went to the local bar with friends for a drink and a game of pool to take a break from your studies, you may have seen images surrounding the pool table, or you might recall a conversation on a particular day with flashes of images of corresponding elements and people. With practice, your senses can be enhanced to where you remember the smell of the fish and chips that you ordered or the sound of laughter with other people that were present. This is an example of the marvelous power of creation. You recreated an experience in your mind's eye and brought it forth even though it may have been twenty years ago. The images can be as real and clear as if it was last week.

The brilliance of your internal vision is that your brain doesn't know the difference between what you are experiencing in the present moment and what you created and saw in your mind's eye. By focusing your visual attention on wellness rather than illness your brain will process this as a reality and send signals throughout your body to be in alignment with this reality. Every cell of your body will instantly respond to these signals.

In my own inner image, I could see myself hiking with my family, seeing the beautiful view at the top of the summit and breathing in the fresh air. I always looked healthy, happy, and strong—with my body toned and in possession of an abundance of energy to literally run up the trail if I desired. Each person's vision of what health means to them is theirs to design. You may not desire to hike a mountain. In fact, you may be at the point in your healing journey where to visualize walking around the block would feel like a huge milestone. Then again, you may have the desire to run a marathon. Crafting your life is specific to YOU. If you visually focus on specific details of your healing, every aspect of your life begins to respond and realign.

I have a dear friend that was a patient of my husband's for many years. When he first met her, she told him that her goal was to be able to interact with her young children a few hours each day. This seemed like an almost impossible goal, given that she was very ill, had endured multiple surgeries, and was barely interacting with her family at all. As most people that have endured years of personal struggle can attest, there are many aspects of life that become illuminated that are often taken for granted. A stay-at-home mother may take for granted what a blessing it is to interact with her children each day, but if you spend your days in bed, this interaction could almost be an impossible feat. My friend held onto the image of what being a mom meant for her: preparing meals, playing with her children, and assisting with homework. Thanks to the healing support from my husband and using supplements that he advised, she was able to get off of fourteen medications. Within two years she was fully interacting with her children, thriving as a real estate agent, and contributing to her household as the breadwinner!

The power of sight arises from the ability to hold an image within your mind and to visualize the elements involved in its creation. To improve your ability to visualize, you will need to release emotions of fear and scarcity, and calm your thoughts and physical activity. There is a bridge between the conscious and the subconscious mind that naturally takes place twice each day, within the first fifteen to twenty minutes of waking and just as you are drifting back to sleep at the end of the day. You can also deliberately access this state of awareness through meditation. During these times your brain activity is in the state of creation and it is easier to access the subconscious mind.

One of the struggles that many people experience is the ability to internally visualize what it is that they desire, especially if what you desire is something that you have never experienced before or feels like it is a polar opposite of your current position. Creating a vision board is a very simple and phenomenal way to internally "see" an external expression.

You may have heard of *The Secret*, the movie that details how wealthy and successful people created a vision board by placing a picture of what they wanted on it—an expensive new car, a new home, vacations to exotic locations, or a loving relationship. While these are great illustrations of what can be accomplished by using a vision board, I want to point out that vision boards don't have to be about amassing greater wealth and a lifestyle of the rich and famous. When you are experiencing illness a vision board can simply be another tool to support you in seeing yourself as well and healed.

You may be thinking, "I've tried that before and it didn't work." And here's the deal: if you taped a picture of a sexy lover, piles of cash, and a mansion with a new Maserati parked in the driveway on a poster board and then after you hung it on your wall you walked away from it thinking, "This probably won't work, but hey, what do I have to lose?" Well, chances are it didn't work. Here's why. Vision boards are meant to be an external representation of an internal vision of what you desire. You can't just post something on the wall and walk away expecting nature to hand you something that you are not aligned with energetically.

By placing an image in front of your physical vision, you are able to see it and create that image within. When you look at that image and memorize the finite details, you can then close your eyes and access the image in your mind's eye by remembering what that image looked like. By holding the vision in your mind's eye and repeating this process over and over you begin to see outside evidence that this is possible and, eventually, start to believe it to be true.

It is at this time that the shift takes place. Once your brain sees the image as a reality it becomes a belief. Having this belief shifts your vibrations into alignment with that which you desire. Once you are in alignment you cannot fail at bringing it into fruition.

Having something to see externally will support your abilities to internally visualize. If you desire a new relationship, a new skill, better finances, a new job, and abundant health, then find an image that represents your desired outcome—and keep that image close to you. You can hang it up on a vision board or use it as a screen background on your phone. Keep this vision board visible. You may think others will judge you if they see a vision board hanging next to your bed and feel inclined to hide it by hanging it in the closet. Energetically, this is hiding from your desires. I'm not implying that you need to brag about it, just don't hide it. Spend time with these images every day to integrate them into your subconscious mind. Enhance your visual acuity by integrating your other senses. Touch, taste, hear, and feel what you see in that image as if it is the life that you are living right now. The more time you spend holding your image internally the quicker you will attract it externally.

Remember to manage the other elements of creation—thoughts, words, and emotions—in relationship to your vision. If you are looking at an image of you in a loving relationship while having thoughts that this will never happen and feeling resentful that nobody has ever loved you like that before, then you are reminding your brain that it is not safe to bring it to you. But, if you hold an image of you traveling to exotic places with your partner and feel excitement and joy, while declaring out loud, "I am in a loving, supportive, and fun relationship," while thinking about and feeling all the fun things that you will do together, you are maximizing your creation potential.

EMOTIONS

If visualization is the train of creation, then emotions are the conductor. Emotions are the driving force that can move energy, bringing to you what you desire. On the flip side, emotions can also push your desires further away. Remember, certain areas of your brain have the primary role of keeping you safe. If you are experiencing emotions of fear, anxiety, or angst when engaged in thought about what you are trying to create on the conscious level, your subconscious mind picks up on these signals and alarms the bell. Abort! This is not a safe territory.

Emotions are a beautiful part of being alive but they can also be a very painful aspect as well. It sucks to feel low, hopeless, anxious, depressed, or out of sorts. And when you're sick, being in a negative emotional state adds to the already heavy burden of physical challenges.

Anyone that has struggled with depression can attest to the challenges in finding hope and clarity. It becomes an uphill battle to pull yourself out of a heavy emotional state because emotions are like magnets—you attract more of the same. It takes awareness and consistent effort to pull yourself out of the dumps into a feeling of possibility. This is why, when you are in a grumpy mood or feel angry and someone tries to lift your spirits, it only annoys you. Your negative emotional state overrides the benefit of doing anything about it, even though it doesn't feel good to feel the way you do.

Negative emotions are caused by thinking about or responding to something in your life that you don't want. If unresolved, these negative emotions are eventually expressed as physical pain. By being conscious of when these negative emotions arise, and switching your attention to something you desire, you can break the chain of a negative emotional spiral. If you don't know how to articulate your emotions toward a desire, then focus on something that you enjoy. I'm not suggesting that you attempt to force your thoughts from misery and pain to the feeling of dancing on the ceiling because it won't feel real and is not sustaining. It may help for you to recognize that you, as an individual, are not the emotion, but rather someone that is feeling an emotion. Having this understanding can feel empowering in emotional management.

When I have caught myself in a downward emotional spiral, fearing that I was never going to heal, I was acutely aware that my physical pain was intensified. I became edgy with people around me and fearful thoughts ran out of control. I knew that managing my emotions was going to be one of the hardest things that I needed to do in my healing experience and the most valuable. It took constant vigilance and awareness to catch the negative emotions and instantly shift my thoughts by remembering that I have felt healthy before—remembering that my soul knows strength, health, and vitality. By holding my attention on this memory and what it felt like to be healthy, I was reminded that it was possible to do it again.

Negative emotions that build up in the body rarely leave the physical body on their own. Stored within our body's energetic field, they are tangible and always present in disease. Suppressed negative emotions build up over time and become dangerous to our health. These built-up negative emotions limit the energetic flow of the body and affect the lymphatic system, the elimination system, and blood, and they block the ability to receive energetic healing.

According to Dr. Candace Pert, all of the body systems are connected and coordinated by emotion-laden, information-carrying molecules. These molecules cross-communicate throughout every system in the body, from the digestive system to the nervous system and even the immune system. In Dr. Pert's book, *Everything You Need to Know to Feel Go(o)d,* she describes how this communication between cells takes place throughout the body and brain, involving intelligence and emotion to create one entity she calls the "bodymind." Dr. Pert's scientific research shows how emotions are the key to how energy heals, how mind becomes matter, and how we can create our own reality. Not only are emotions the driving force to move your thoughts, vision, and words into creation but the rate at which you arrive at the new state of your creation is based upon your ability to access the emotional frequency of that which you desire.

When we delve into emotions and the power emotional energy has in healing the body, there may be an overlapping question that if your body can heal based upon your emotional state, then does that mean your emotional state caused your illness or disease in the first place? Wow! Talk about putting a lot of pressure on yourself. I feel that it's healthier to come from the understanding that there are many elements that co-create your state of wellness, not all of which are your doing. However, taking the reins on what you do have control over in your co-creating capacity is always a smart move.

To gain a deeper understanding of how magical the human body is and how important emotions are to your health, let's look at the basis of biochemistry as described by Dr. Pert. There are two components that make up the bodymind communication system: receptors and ligands. Virtually every cell in the body has thousands of tiny structures which are called receptors. These receptors pick up signals coming to them from the surrounding space. Once the receptors receive a signal, the information is transferred to deep within the cell's interior, initiating key processes. This information directs cell division and growth, cell migration for attacking enemies and making repairs, and cell metabolism to conserve or spend energy. The signal, which comes from other cells throughout the body, is carried by an informational substance, providing the infrastructure for communication throughout the bodymind and is known to you and me as hormones, neurotransmitters, and peptides. In the science world it is referred to as ligands. Ligands are responsible for 98 percent of all data transfer in the body and brain. Peptides are ligands consisting of the string of amino acids joined together. According to Dr. Pert, there are over two hundred peptides mapped in the brain and body, each one sounding a complex emotional chord such as bliss, hunger, anger, relaxation, or satiety when their signals are received by the cell. Most ligands have chemical equivalents that can be found outside the body, such as marijuana, alcohol, and caffeine. These peptides float around until they find their perfect match, the receptors. Each receptor is specifically shaped to fit only one ligand.

The new understanding of the relationship between ligands and receptors involves "vibratory attraction." According to this concept, the receptors on the surface of a cell are in a constant state of flux, creating a vibration that resonates with its match. Vibrating at the same frequency, they begin to resonate together and this creates a force of attraction, striking an emotional chord as they bind. This attracting vibration is the emotion, and the connection of peptide to receptor is the manifestation of the feeling of the emotion in the physical world. Dr. Pert goes on to explain that the receptors are dynamic molecular targets, modulating our physiology in response to our experience. Emotions influence the molecules, which in turn affect how we feel. In other words, our physical body can be changed by the emotions we experience.

Science has also now proven that receptors are often clumped together in tight, multiple complexes, forming the walls leading into the interior of the cell, opening and closing with a rhythmic, pumping action. As they move, these channels let substances in and out of the cell, setting up an electrical current which courses throughout the bodymind. This current influences the firing of neurons in the brain and determines brain cell activation—directly affecting how you think! So, what you experience as a feeling is the actual vibrational dance of peptides binding to their receptors.

I know that was a lot of information but it's incredibly valuable. Take a deep breath and stay with me…

Emotions are the one element of creation that you not only have to manage from this point on in order to heal, but also from the point of the past. You need to release the emotions that have been held up inside of your body. Many people intuitively strive for emotional healing by trying to soothe internal sensations with external stuff, like buying a new car, or a larger home, or more clothes and jewelry. This is never sustaining. It offers a momentary state of elation but that feeling leaves very quickly. Emotional healing will never come from attaining more in the outer world. It is a releasing of the internal pain that allows healing to take place.

Today, we live in a world of emotional turmoil. Many physicians are now recognizing the possibility that a number of diseases are caused by emotions that are linked back to fetal development in the womb. Negative emotions that have been held onto may have compromised the immune system or genetic structuring, causing children to have a weakened immune response.

There are few things in life that match the trauma of a diagnosis of a terminal illness or knowing that something is desperately wrong with your body and not knowing how to fix it. It's healthy to momentarily feel negative emotions and give yourself permission to process it all. But when your body is not responding in the way that you feel that it should, emotions build up and you will look toward the nearest target to attack, which will often be your own body. Feelings of physical pain, not responding to treatments, or wounds not healing can cause feelings of anger and a sense of betrayal by your body.

No one is their optimal self when they don't feel good. And when I was sick, I felt miserable. Every time I had the slightest setback with my health, my emotions went out of control. Old "what if" stories clamored for my attention—fear and a sense of not feeling supported would rise to the surface.

When I had experienced many months of incredible levels of physical pain I felt angry and frustrated. I wanted to act out and hit my belly. I felt so many emotions and believed that I didn't want to reside in my body anymore. How could I trust a body that was doing everything wrong when I was doing all that I could to heal? I knew in these moments that I wasn't healing my body but rather inflicting more negativity and pain onto myself. It became more apparent that for me to heal on the physical level I needed to treat my body with compassion. To be gentle and forgiving. To speak and think kindly toward the body that has suffered.

Emotions are in constant motion much like the ocean tide. Fear of being in more pain and not knowing if I could handle the threshold often caused me greater anxiety. Much like hearing about the death of a loved one, fearing your own demise can make your body go numb. While some people completely shut down from sharing how they feel, others feel a need to keep telling anyone that will listen what is going on with them. When you see someone who is repeatedly telling stories about their trauma, what their brains are trying to do is make peace in their mind. It's like their brains have short-circuited a section of time and they're still trying to put pieces back together.

You may be familiar with the phrase that time heals all wounds. This is the passive response to healing, where thinking that if you allow enough time to pass that eventually your body will no longer hold the emotional charge that it had before. I can assure you, though, that emotions are not limited to time and space. You may know this if you have experienced an incident that triggers you emotionally from your past, such as a photo, a scent of perfume, or being in a similar environment as the original emotional incident and it takes you right back into the emotional charge that you had before.

Releasing negative emotions is a valuable tool for healing. I will go into more detail on ways to release negative emotions in chapter 9, but here are a few of my favorite powerful emotional release options:

- **Write and destroy:** Grab some paper and start writing about the negative emotions you're feeling. Don't hold back. Begin by writing "I feel…" and then just let it rip. As you do this, remember, you are an individual that is feeling emotions—you are not the emotion itself. This is a powerful way to release those emotions and is a much healthier dumping ground than unloading on loved ones and caregivers. This is for your eyes only. No dumping on or sharing with others. Continue to write until you have released the negative emotions. Once you are finished you will want to get rid of it. After all, these are emotions that you released and you don't want them back. Destroy the paper by either tearing it, shredding it, burning it, or wadding it up and throwing it in the trash.

- **Clear out physical clutter:** This is one of my favorite techniques when I have built up emotions. I believe that internal clutter is represented by the external clutter around us. Everything holds energy. As you are transitioning into a healthier internal state it's a good idea to get rid of things that are no longer a good fit for who you are. The first place to start is your bedroom, or the place you spend the most time. Keep your nightstand in order. Don't have piles of clothes, books, medical paperwork, or bottles of pills cluttered around your bed. All of these are excess weight that is holding you down. Clean out drawers, closets, and the rooms you spend the most time in. If you don't have the strength to do this on your own, enlist someone to help. Get rid of anything that causes a negative emotional charge. By creating order, you are healing your personal environment and opening space to heal your internal environment as well.

- **Physical exercise:** Physical movement helps the emotions move too, just be responsible and don't push yourself so hard physically that you cause yourself to have setbacks in health. It is still a great idea to move and exercise at a level that builds some endurance, even if just a little.

- **Crying:** Crying relieves tension and stress in the body and helps to improve your mood. Go ahead, let it all out. Watch a chick flick or listen to sad music. Do whatever it takes to pull those emotions up and out with a good cry fest.

- **Get outside:** A change of scenery is refreshing. Fresh air and being in nature can cause you to shift the heaviness that you feel. Go for a drive up a mountain or to a park, hiking trail, river, or lake. Find a tree to talk to and share all the negative emotions that you have been feeling. Fresh air always helps you feel better.

Once you have let out negative emotions there will be empty space in your energetic field. Refill that space with positive emotions to block the negative ones from coming back in. Here are a few ideas:

- **Dance:** You know that expression, dance as if no one is watching? That is exactly what you do. Find two or three of your favorite upbeat songs. Turn up the music and start moving your body.

Chapter 6 - Elements of Creation

Music is an amazing way to help move emotions.

- **Connect to God:** You can do this in prayer or just in a quiet space. Visualize yourself connecting to something much larger than you that encompasses you in love and support.

- **Mirror talk:** Have a heart to heart conversation with yourself while looking in the mirror. Give yourself encouraging support. Rather than looking for flaws, your only purpose is to express love and kindness and deliver a good pep talk to yourself.

- **Choose your mood:** Make a list of all the uplifting and positive emotions you would like, drawing upon the emotions listed below if you need some inspiration. Just make sure that the emotions you choose are positive and uplifting. Once you have your list, wake up every morning and choose how you will feel. We may not have control over our environment and experiences but we do have control over how we respond to them. Choose between one and five emotions that you will have throughout the day. Once you choose your mood, hold the line and allow nothing to change how you feel. Keep your list next to where you sleep so that you can see it first thing in the morning and decide how you are going to embrace the day. Feel free to continue to add to your list when other emotions and attributes that you want to integrate into your life show up. You may want to choose to feel:

Blissful	Hopeful	Energetic	Radiant	Empowered	Happy
Faithful	Clear	Vibrant	Healthy	Victorious	Loving
Valiant	Cheerful	Brave	Grateful	Courageous	Triumphant
Priceless	Intuitive	Balanced	Confident	Joyful	Enthusiastic
Inspired	Strong	Passionate	Fun	Spiritual	Fearless
Peaceful	Rested	Optimistic	Lovable	Calm	Forgiving
Connected	Uplifted	Present	Relaxed	Enlightened	Trusting
Patient	Motivated	Purposeful	Responsive	Committed	Supported

- **Keep a self-gratitude list:** Write out all of the positive qualities that you have. Keep this list close and read it each day—especially when you are feeling low. Continue to add to the list as you think of more aspects of your amazingness.

Only allow positive influences into your life. If you need to, have a friend or partner protect you from that overbearing mother-in-law who thinks you should get up and work it off or the nosy neighbor who thinks you are trying to get everyone to feel sorry for you. Shut that noise out. There is always going to be somebody who has an opinion about how you're living your life. Those are not the people that you want to spend your time with.

Remember that you cannot have that which is not a match to you vibrationally. To support healing, you will need to get your body to vibrationally match the health you seek, and the quickest way to adjust your vibration is through emotions. It is not a matter of pretending to be happy when you are not, but it is quite simple. I never could force a smile when I felt angry and pretend to be "fine." BUT, I can recall a time when I felt happy and access the physical and emotional sensations of that feeling. By holding my attention on the emotion, I am able to recalibrate my vibration.

Nearly every person has experienced a level of vibrancy and health at some point. This means that your body knows how to feel that way, and your job now is to access it. Instead of feeling jealousy, envy, anger, or resentment when you see someone that is healthy and vibrant and enjoying their life, tune in to what that must feel like for them to feel that way. Ask yourself, "What would I do right now if my body was strong, healthy, free of pain, energetic, and vibrant? What thoughts would I have about myself and others? How would I engage with others if my body was how I desire it to be?"

Once you have accessed your co-creating powers of thoughts, vision, words, and emotions, play the story out in your mind with everything that you have. Utilize all your senses. As an example, imagine if you were a bird. Again, access how you would think, what you would see, and how you would feel as you fly above the world. Would you perch on a telephone pole overlooking the park, watching and listening to children play soccer? Or, fly over the homes and see different families interacting in their backyards, and see everyday mechanics of the world—cars on the roads, dogs barking as they pass? You may have flown in an airplane and therefore, can access visual images of what it's like to be above the rest of the world, but you have never flown like a bird. I bet you can imagine it, right?

Now, do this for yourself in regards to your health. Imagine what it feels like to be what you desire. Visualize yourself as healthy and vibrant, accessing the emotional components of someone who enjoys good health. The most crucial aspect is to feel the emotion and be a vibrational match to health—repeatedly. This is not a one-time experience. The more attention you give to this creation, the more you draw it toward you. Spend time every day in this imagery.

A good time to practice visualizations is in the first few moments upon awakening. Before you remember to focus on your challenges, spend ten to twenty minutes engaging your senses in the *feeling* of health and vibrancy. I suggest that you do this before getting out of bed in the morning, otherwise, distractions can occur and increase the tendency to not do so. And remember to choose your mood for the day by making a conscious decision on how you will express yourself. If you have doctor appointments planned, decide to bring joy and optimism with you. If you are expecting company later in the day, decide to have fun and engage in laughter.

Imagine what it feels like to enjoy favorite activities such as hiking, playing with children, or traveling with your best friend. Think, feel, and visualize an ideal day for yourself. You can even record yourself describing the perfect day in every detail, including how you feel and listen to this recording each morning. The more attention and detail you give to creating these experiences in your vibration, the quicker you will begin to believe and achieve them.

As you move through your day, remember your responsibility as co-creator of your own universe. Remember your power to affect your reality through your thoughts, words, vision, and emotions. Choose your mood about this as well. Don't think of this as drudgery, as one more responsibility weighing you down. Get excited about hope and possibilities. Make it a game by setting a goal in maintaining a positive attitude. Then, use this power to move yourself toward healing and wholeness.

CHAPTER 7

Nutrition

Each of us are unique individuals who require different levels of nutrition. In today's fast-paced and hurried lifestyle we have set ourselves up for an environment where many of our meals are eaten on the go. We live in an instant gratification world of microwaved and prepackaged food where speed and efficiency have overtaken nutritional quality. Eating your dinner out of a paper bag while driving to your next errand has become second nature to many of us and a common scene on the road. This behavior completely removes awareness from our relationship with food.

In our Western culture, there is often a reference to the Standard American Diet, which typically consists of a high level of refined flour, red meat, artificial sweeteners, trans fats, and salt. Standard American Diet meals are predominantly in the form of prepackaged or fast foods that are void of life and nutrition. This diet is also sometimes referred to by its acronym—SAD—because the Standard American Diet often contains a sadly limited amount of healthy foods like fresh fruits, vegetables, fish, and whole grains. Very few Americans eat the recommended amount of vegetables. Unfortunately, the demographic eating the least vegetables is teenagers, with nearly half of their vegetable intake being potatoes and tomatoes. Fries and ketchup, anyone?

From a food industry perspective, it comes down to two key elements: money and public demand. Food manufacturing is like any other business. To thrive and be successful, you need to provide what the public wants. Food manufacturers pour billions of dollars toward marketing and production of their products. Providing food that looks appealing and tastes good ensures a higher consumer base, and reaching these goals profitably often results in food that no longer qualifies as quality nourishment and energy for the body.

Food production companies keep a sharp eye on the latest health trends—again, because of public demand. When obesity was on the incline there was a huge shift in processed foods marketed as fat-free. Many health professionals now agree this was not in the public's best interest as far as their health was concerned, pointing out that our bodies need dietary fats for energy and to absorb nutrients. With the increase in diabetes came an alarming increase of sugar alternatives marketed as sugar-free. Many people thought they hit the jackpot with this one but the chemical-laden alternatives, including aspartame, in these sugar-free products have horrible effects on the body.

I am included in the demographic following the latest craze, going gluten-free. Although I have never been medically diagnosed with celiac disease, I do know my body and how I react to gluten-containing grains. I have regained my health in every area except my ability to eat gluten-containing foods. If I were to be contaminated with even a trace amount of gluten I would have a severe reaction of vomiting, diarrhea, severe shaking, bloating, and a few days of nausea and inflammation. Not fun.

In 2012 there were very few gluten-free options available in restaurants and grocery stores, and the few gluten-free items that were available had a horrible consistency and lacked nutrients and taste. Many people felt that it was just another fad and it was very challenging for me to have restaurant servers take me seriously. I was often treated as a burden that the restaurant staff had to "deal with." It was hard enough for me to keep myself safe in my home environment with my family who still continued to eat gluten-containing foods and it became crucial for me to only eat food that I prepared so that I could limit the possibility of getting contaminated. Because of my extreme reactions, "gluten-free" are the first words I look for on any food items that I purchase.

I am incredibly grateful for the health practitioners and nutritionists that are paving the way for a greater understanding of the impact of gluten in our diet, and for food companies that properly label allergens, which saves me time in the grocery aisle.

Allergies and food sensitivities have skyrocketed, causing a great debate as to the root of the problem. Remember the days when nearly every child had a peanut butter and jelly sandwich for school lunch? Now, there are signs posted in classrooms and school cafeterias designating them as peanut-free zones. For generations, bread has been a staple in most homes around the world. While awareness of gluten-free diets is spreading, it is still challenging for me to travel or go out to dinner with friends who don't understand the severity of any possible reactions.

In many restaurants, it is typical for the server to place a basket of bread on the table as soon as you are seated, unless you are at a Mexican restaurant, where you would be offered a bowl of chips and salsa—a whole other issue, in and of itself. Nearly all corn chips are produced using genetically modified corn and oil. Countless studies link the damaging effects of genetically modified organisms (GMO) foods to systemic health concerns, including inflammation and an imbalance in our gut bacteria. I know… I know… I just opened Pandora's box mentioning GMOs. There are supporters of GMO foods claiming they solve world hunger by providing more efficient crops. I and many others will attest, though, that GMOs are a key player in most, if not all, conditions labeled as autoimmune disease, digestive problems, and a host of other health conditions that we deal with today. These genetically modified foods have thrown us into a chemical lab station just about as far away as possible from the food values that have supported health for thousands of years. We all too often overlook the purpose of food as a way to nourish our cells and give our bodies what they need for energy and regeneration.

Thankfully, I was raised in a home where most of our meals came directly out of the garden. As a family, we couldn't afford the luxuries of fast food chains or restaurants. In fact, the first time I ever ate at a restaurant was when I was nine years old. My aunts took me and my siblings for the summer to Canada to see extended family while my parents processed their divorce. It was such a novelty to sit at a restaurant table and order pancakes while my sister next to me ordered waffles and my aunt had an omelet. In my innocent mind, I was taking in the wonder of it all, marveling how each person could order exactly what they desired and someone would magically appear from behind the swinging door with a plate, fulfilling their request.

That following school year was challenging for me as I witnessed the pain that my parents were going through during their divorce. With the instability of my home life, I tried to find comfort and stability at school. I wanted my teacher to love me as much as I loved her and I tried very hard to make her happy. Her classroom was similar to any other classroom in elementary schools across the country. In the back corner was a large colorful rug where the students would sit in a circle while our teacher entranced us as she read from a great book. On the wall behind her was a poster of the food pyramid. I would often stare at the poster as I lost myself in the latest adventure we were reading.

I enjoyed school. Especially fun was how my teacher made transitions from one activity to another. Instead of having twenty-four students clamoring at once to their desk she would make it a game. Some days she would say things like, "Whoever is wearing tennis shoes can go back to their desk." Or, "Whoever is wearing a blue shirt." One day, we were learning about nutrition and the food pyramid on the poster. My teacher excused us back to our seats with, "Whoever had eggs for breakfast can go back to their seat." A few of my peers got up. She went through the typical breakfast categories of cereal, pancakes, waffles, and toast. This continued until I was the last one sitting at the rug. I felt embarrassed because I hadn't eaten breakfast that morning and was mad at myself for not thinking quicker. Why didn't I just stand up with one of the breakfast options? My teacher asked me what I had for breakfast. I responded that I didn't eat breakfast that morning. She looked at me with pity and told me to go back to my seat. In that moment of shame and embarrassment, I decided to pay more attention to food—not because as a nine-year-old I knew the value of nutrient-dense foods, but more to protect myself from embarrassment again. If my teacher ever asked what I had for breakfast I would be ready.

Choosing to become a conscious eater involves having an awareness of what you are eating and where your food comes from. This may seem to be basic knowledge and yet very few people eat consciously. Unfortunately, we are continually bombarded with the new latest health study that conflicts with the last health study that we just jumped on board with! Most fast food chains and grocery stores offer a variety of "foods" that are laden with excitotoxins and added chemicals that confuse the body, forcing us to become sleuths in label reading and to pay attention to healthy keywords such as antioxidants, superfood, and omega 3s, in the hope to get the most bang for our buck.

Our health is directly related to the quality and type of food that we eat, which affects our mood, hormone balance, and sense of well-being. As essential as quality nutrition is to our bodies, what we eat is also more than that; the act of eating is a social and spiritual experience. Meals are meant to be a time when the family comes together to reconnect and engage in one another's lives. Traditionally, families share the same meal but with the barrage of commercials geared toward children and the onslaught of food sensitivities, personal preferences, and allergen restrictions, there are often as many meals on the table as people around it.

Young children of today are growing up in an environment where they and their peers order from a separate menu than their parents, with limited options including chicken nuggets, corn dogs, mac and cheese, mini pizzas, and hamburgers. As a mother of young children, my first thoughts in the morning are often, "What am I going to fix for dinner tonight?" I feel the same frustration and pressure that other parents feel when everyone is tired and hungry and looking to me to feed them. And even though my children eat cheeseburgers, hot dogs, fruit snacks, pizza, chicken nuggets, french fries, and potato chips, I try to source these items responsibly, ensuring that the meat is free of antibiotics and hormones, grass fed rather than grain fed, and raised in a humane manner. I buy organic and non-GMO as much as possible and limit processed foods and sugar intake. I feel that it is my responsibility to educate my children to recognize the correlation between what we eat and how we feel. To reflect on our food choices and how they affect our bellies, energy level, and elimination.

In my own healing paradigm, my key focus revolved around my gut and I knew that I was not alone. Everywhere I turned there were more conversations about gut health and gastrointestinal issues than ever before. Symptoms included irritable bowel syndrome, cramping, constipation, diarrhea, bloating, and excessive gas. There were so many people that were also suffering with these physical symptoms that a new language began to appear in our everyday conversations that we hadn't heard of ten years ago—words like leaky gut, autoimmune, and gluten intolerance. More and more people became likely to respond with "me too" when a friend shared her health challenges rather than just offering a sympathetic ear.

One of the biggest challenges to my health was a constant barrage on my system from leaky gut. Leaky gut, or intestinal permeability, causes proteins and carbohydrates to be released into the bloodstream. This triggered an "autoimmune" response causing inflammation throughout my body. There were several times that I had been inadvertently contaminated by a food that I was reactive to and when this happened I would experience severe inflammation, bloating, and several days with fatigue and intestinal distress. My healing had to begin at the cellular level by repairing my digestive system.

Your gut is not only the core of your physical body, but literally, the core of your health as well. Seventy percent of our immune system is located in the lining of the gut, where many autoimmune issues are rooted from a compromised gut wall. Various inflammatory foods such as refined sugar, gluten, and dairy can damage the gut lining, thereby setting up an immune reaction.

Your gut and brain are in constant communication and affect every level of your body. The gut microbiome is home to trillions of microorganisms. The microbiome has more impact on your health than your genetics—influencing your weight, ability to focus, energy levels, emotions, sleep patterns, and physical pain, and can contribute to chronic health conditions. Your microbiome is uniquely you. In fact, only 5 percent of your gut microorganisms are the same as anyone else's. If you nourish these organisms with the right foods and make healthy lifestyle choices, you can boost your overall wellness and potentially prevent disease.

The first step to repairing a leaky gut and reaching optimal digestive health is to eliminate the foods that are contributing to your symptoms. Eliminate all processed foods, sugar, and foods that you react to, which may include corn, eggs, dairy, soy, gluten, peanuts, tree nuts, fish, and shellfish. In fact, ninety percent of allergic reactions to food are from those nine categories. Work with a healing practitioner, if possible, to determine whether you have toxic heavy metal overload, viruses, parasites, or candida overgrowth. My husband, Scott Werner, has supported thousands of people around the world by guiding them through the process of detoxing, providing intuitive readings, and recommending nutritional supplements. His book *Take Back Your Health* provides the necessary information for detoxing the body and ridding yourself of parasites, virus, candida, and heavy metals.

Whether you are healing from a chronic illness or not, it is a good idea to implement a healthy nutritional lifestyle. Consider making small adjustments that you can stick to. When it comes to healing, there is no time better than right now to make a positive impact on your health. At the very least, increase live food by incorporating more organic fruits and vegetables into your diet. Proper assimilation of nutrients is also incredibly important. Listen to your body and notice how you respond to the foods that you eat. Be certain if you eat gluten proteins that you can digest them properly. Notice if you have any bloating, gas, cramping, brain fog, or joint inflammation. These are all indicators that you are not digesting your food properly. If this is the case, then you need to increase your intake of digestive enzymes and integrate more traditional food preparation techniques such as soaking and fermentation. By soaking grains, beans, nuts, and seeds prior to eating them you are making the digestion process much easier on your body because it doesn't have to work so hard to digest these foods. Sprouting removes the antinutrients that are in nuts and beans and proper fermentation makes foods more bioavailable for nutrient assimilation.

Create a supportive environment for digestion. Sit down at the table and take time to enjoy the experience, free of your phone and television. Make the cooking experience a mindful and enjoyable one. Create memories with family in the kitchen by exploring new recipes that are healing and supportive to your well-being. My husband and I love to chop vegetables and work together while we prepare meals with enjoyable music in the background to enhance the environment.

Capitalize on days when you have more energy by preparing multiple meals in advance and freeze them for days that you don't feel well or have a busy schedule. I often bake up a batch of sweet potatoes or beets so they can be warmed up within a few minutes. I make muffins that I can eat throughout the week and a variety of soups that are easy to warm up. Add supplements, digestive enzymes, and superfoods such as avocados, blueberries, almonds, coconut, and sweet potatoes into your diet plan. Enjoy a wide variety of local produce that is in season and add in omega-3-rich fish such as wild salmon.

Also, if you want to get to the bare bones (pun intended) of the healing process and create an ideal healing environment in the gut, I suggest including bone broth in your daily life.

BONE BROTH AND GUT HEALING

Bone broth has recently regained its rightful place at the top of the healing spectrum. In addition to being a staple in many kitchens for its culinary benefits, bone broth has also had a long and rich history of medicinal use. With all the attention given recently to bone broth in virtually all healing circles, quality bone broth is now available at most health food stores or online—a must for convenience when you feel too weak or busy to make your own. Making your own broth, however, is simple and more affordable.

Bone broth is versatile and relevant for every stage of life and wellness, and is a significant player in healing and repair in everything from recovery after giving birth to recovery from surgery. Bone broth is soothing to the system when it feels challenging to eat and you have no appetite, and fuels your body with resources required to recover faster and heal stronger.

Drinking bone broth provides a nutritionally dense and soothing replacement to eating foods that are hard to break down, allowing a weakened digestive system time to heal. Known for containing a high level of valuable nutrients, bone broth made with quality sourced bones has been used by cultures around the world to do more than support digestive health. Bone broth also improves immune function, heals damaged joints and ligaments, and mineralizes bones and teeth. Unlike meats and vegetables, bone broth contains a significant amount of the healthy amino acids that bones, marrow, and connective tissue are rich in. When slow simmered for hours, these healthy proteins and amino acids soak into the bone broth and make their way into your body.

The most common base for bone broth in the Western world is quality sourced beef or chicken. Think chicken noodle soup without the noodles. But, you can use virtually any animal bones, including fish, wild game, and bison, as your base or, if you are vegetarian, quality sourced eggshells are a healthy substitute.

Why bones? Bones are made up of minerals and amino acids, including calcium, magnesium, collagen, chondroitin sulfates, and glucosamine. Slowly simmering bones, cartilage, and organ meat along with a small amount of acid, such as lemon or vinegar, in water for eight to twenty-four hours, depending on the bones used, is all that you need to create a rich and delicious broth. This process slowly breaks down the bones into a nutritionally dense and easily digestible healing superfood. By cooking on low heat, valuable nutrients such as glutamine, glycine, glucosamine, collagen, and calcium soak into the broth. This long cooking process ensures that the nutrients and amino acids in the bones break down to create a broth that is high in protein and other nutrients and is easily digestible.

The gut is the seat of the immune system and the gateway to health; therefore, a damaged gut can be a trigger for autoimmunity and systemic breakdown. A compromised gut lining also prevents efficient nutrient absorption. Gut imbalances can result from multiple factors—including pathogens, emotional and physical stress, overuse of antibiotics that kill off both the bad and good bacteria in your gut, and repeated ingestion of foods that cause chronic gut inflammation—and create an internal environment that makes losing weight, recovering from illness or surgery, and having an abundance of energy challenging.

Bone broth is a time-tested home remedy for both acute and chronic gut distress. Its therapeutic properties are the result of its many minerals, vitamins, and easily assimilated amino acids leached from the vegetables, herbs, and bones of healthy, pastured animals.

Our bodies expend a lot of energy replacing the intestinal lining every few days. The amino acids, fats, and trace minerals found in bone broth are essential components in this process and support the health of your gut. When the gut isn't healthy, the immune system isn't healthy, and an unhealthy immune system increases the risk of developing any type of illness, including autoimmunity. Autoimmunity and gut health are mutually inclusive health concerns. Autoimmune disease is characterized by an overactive immune system responding to foreign particles from the intestines sneaking past the gut wall into the bloodstream. As intestinal permeability (leaky gut) is reduced and less foreign particles pass into the blood stream, inflammation decreases and autoimmune conditions not only improve but can also be completely healed. Repairing a leaky gut opens the door for improved mental clarity, increased energy, reduced joint pain, and decreased inflammation.

We've touched on leaky gut briefly, but since leaky gut can have profound health implications, I'd like to take a moment to look at it in greater detail. Leaky gut syndrome refers to a separation between the tight junctions of your intestinal lining, which creates holes that allow your body to release potentially harmful substances and waste that would otherwise be processed via natural elimination. Stress, parasites, infections, alcohol, smoking, inflammation, and consuming the Standard American Diet of processed foods and chemicals all weaken the lining of the gut—and the implications of this are massive. Weakening the lining of the gut weakens your immune system and causes inflammation, food intolerances, food cravings, and hormonal imbalances, which can eventually lead to an autoimmune diagnosis. Leaky gut and systemic inflammation are closely associated with autoimmune conditions across the board.

Bone broth provides a way of healing and sealing leaky gut and maintaining healthy gut flora to help correct digestive disturbances, multiple sclerosis, Crohn's disease, and all forms of autoimmunity. My dear friend Sarica Cernohous, a master of traditional food preparation, taught me a catchphrase regarding the proper preparation of bone broth: "low and slow to heal and seal." By cooking on low heat over time you are able to keep the protein structure from breaking down and maintain the high level of amino acid content, which helps heal the tight junctions of the intestinal lining and reverses leaky gut and many other digestive issues. By healing and sealing the intestinal lining, an environment is created to support you in overcoming food intolerance and allergies, improve joint health, and boost the immune system. Studies also show that bone broth helps heal disorders like asthma and arthritis thanks to the high levels of proteins and amino acids present in bones and bone marrow.

Animal bones, skin, fascia, tendons, ligaments and connective tissues contain a protein called collagen, which is the primary structural protein in the human body. When collagen is cooked to make bone broth it becomes gelatin. Gelatin is a powerhouse loaded in protein that is high in antioxidants and known for healing gut health, improving metabolism, and strengthening your immune system. It protects and heals the mucosal lining of the digestive tract that aids in the absorption of nutrients.

What makes gelatin so incredibly powerful are the four amino acids within its structure: proline, glycine, arginine, and glutamine. These amino acids are very easily assimilated by the body, making them a crucial component in healing, restoration, and preventive care, especially when you need to make nutrient absorption easier. Here is some information about each of these amino acids and what role they perform in healing:

- **Glutamine:** Glutamine restores the integrity of your intestinal wall by rebuilding the intestinal junctions and helping repair the villi of the small intestines. In addition to helping repair the lining of the gut, this amino acid enhances your immune system, generates glutathione (a key antioxidant necessary for liver detoxification), and curbs sugar cravings. In addition, glutamine also crosses the blood-brain barrier, making broth a tremendous support in recovering from depression, anxiety, and ADHD.

- **Proline:** Proline is found in virtually all plant and animal protein, making deficiency in this amino acid rare; however, it is possible in individuals that consume a high carbohydrate diet that is low in protein and healthy fats. Proline is best known for making skin supple and reducing cellulite, but it is also a key component in leaky gut repair. It regenerates cartilage and is vital to joint health. Proline and glycine are the raw materials your body needs to rebuild tendons, ligaments, and other connective tissues.

- **Glycine:** The glycine content in bone broth is key to reversing chronic health issues related to GI distress by keeping the lining of the intestinal wall intact and strong, which leads to better digestion and assimilation. In addition, glycine aids in the process of liver detoxification. In fact, our bodies require a significant amount of glycine for detoxification of heavy metals such as mercury and lead. Glycine also supports the making of the bile acid that is necessary for your body to break down fat, stimulates stomach acid production, supports the immune system, reduces inflammation, and plays a significant role in wound healing, making bone broth a crucial component in long-term and preventative care.

- **Arginine:** Arginine promotes the production of human growth hormone, boosts metabolism, and assists in restoring proper kidney function. Arginine is another key player in wound repair.

With all these amazing benefits, one may wonder why we weren't all raised on bone broth. Chances are your grandmother made bone broth with the turkey carcass after Thanksgiving or used leftover scraps to improve the taste of her soups. But, in the last fifty years, we opted for convenience and flavor enhancers such as MSG to mimic that homemade meal taste.

Although many of us don't do it often, creating a tasty and nourishing bone broth from scratch remains easy to do, convenient, and inexpensive. Always use high-quality, organically raised bones and organ meat from a source that you trust when making your own bone broth. Animals that are caged and fed GMO grains are not as healthy and thus don't offer the same nutritional profile as their free-range counterparts that live off the land.

To make your own broth, place organ meat and bones in a crockpot and fill with filtered water to approximately 2 inches below the rim. Add either one-fourth cup of apple cider vinegar or the juice from one lemon. This is the acid base required to leach the minerals from the bones. Anything you add at this point is up to you, according to taste preferences. I often add herbs and spices such as bay leaves, parsley, thyme, rosemary, basil, and sea salt. Then turn your crockpot on high and cook for eight to twenty-four hours, depending on which base is used. Feel free to add organic vegetables such as celery, onion, carrots, or garlic toward the end of the cooking process. At the end of your desired cooking time, turn your crockpot down to the warm setting where it can remain for two to three days. You can ladle out warm broth for a nutritious drink throughout the day and refill your crockpot with hot water as needed. The broth will dilute over time but remain delightful. Feel free to add one-fourth teaspoon turmeric to your broth before consuming. The addition tastes wonderful and has great anti-inflammatory qualities.

If you use onion or garlic in your broth, do not share it with your pets, as these foods can be dangerous to their health.

CHAPTER 8

Support Tools

Listed below are specific tools that I used for my healing and continue to use as part of my daily practice. Although there are multiple benefits to these tools they all offer significant support in physical and emotional healing. I encourage you to integrate each of these components into your own healing regimen.

FORGIVENESS AND GRATITUDE

Forgiveness and gratitude may be the most powerful tools for personal transformation. There is not another factor on Earth that can have a greater benefit in freeing your mind and body from the limitations of the past in relation to others and yourself.

I get it—this is a tough one to address. Forgiveness is hard, and forgiving ourselves can often be even harder to do than forgiving others. Why is this? Because we are all hard on ourselves and we happen to reside in the body that is listening to the twenty-four-hour reel of self-deprecating thoughts that are spinning around in our heads. Even though on some level we are giving as much as we can to the world around us, we often hold ourselves to an impossibly high standard. We believe that we should be doing more and be better, stronger, and faster to progress, always wondering what others are thinking about our level of performance. When we are overextended, in physical or emotional pain, and exhausted, rather than having self-compassion, we often beat ourselves up for not having our lives together.

Having unresolved emotions that are still weighing you down robs you of your vital force energy every single day. This energy is crucial for your healing. The problem is you cannot simply forgive the past by deciding to do so. Forgiveness of self and others is a lifelong experience. How many times have you heard the statement, "Just let it go?" Ugh! If it were only that easy! But you cannot release a negative emotion that is not currently emotionally "charged" within you.

Make the decision to forgive your past, including decisions that you've made, relationships you've had, and painful experiences. Choose to have awareness of when negative emotions arise and then look at these as an opportunity to deepen your healing process. Once you have identified an aspect that needs to be forgiven by having a negative emotional response to an experience, then use one of the emotional healing techniques that I have included in this chapter and chapter 9 for healing.

It's a common fear to think that if you forgive someone that you're letting them off the hook. Forgiving someone else's behavior does not give them permission to continue behaving in an unhealthy manner, nor is it validating that what they did was okay. Decide that it is not your role to punish or to create karmic justice. Understand that the weight of unresolved emotions is holding you back until you can recognize a potential gift for your own growth through that experience. Sometimes the gift comes from standing up for ourselves or recognizing our own value. Other times challenging relationships are a way for us to have more clarity about what we don't want in our lives, which gives us the ability to co-create relationships that are more in harmony. Find the gift, give yourself permission to forgive, and release the emotional bondage that is holding you back.

Forgiveness then makes room for more gratitude. Gratitude gives you the opportunity to be the student and the teacher in your life experience. When you open your heart to feeling gratitude you are giving permission to your body to release the disharmony that is within you. By embracing the concept that everything that happens to you is happening for you, you can view each experience as an opportunity for growth and insight. I'm not suggesting that if someone cuts you off while driving on the freeway or if your boss yells at you in a staff meeting, that you simply smile and hold them in your heart with gratitude, believing that they did you a favor. What I am saying is to step back from the actual experience and view the facts based upon all the information that you have. Momentarily disengage from the emotional charge that you may be feeling and listen to the deeper message behind the experience.

Take the above example of being yelled at in a staff meeting in front of your peers. Intuitively ask your higher consciousness what this experience was here to teach you and then be receptive to the answers that come to you. Maybe it was a sign that it's time to move on to a more supportive environment. Maybe it's a wake-up call that you have been playing small in life and this is the catalyst for you to stand up for yourself. Quite possibly this experience could be rooted in a subconscious thought pattern where you have had issues with authority and your higher self is shining light on an opportunity to heal another layer in your subconscious thinking.

When there is an unresolved issue with authority, it is almost always based on a childhood experience, such as being humiliated in front of your peers by your teacher for an incomplete homework assignment. In that moment, you would have felt anger, shame, and resentment as well as embarrassed and judged. The emotional charge of such a traumatizing experience would quickly settle into your subconscious and your mind would always be on the lookout to make sure you never experienced that level of humiliation again. Over the years, you try to keep others happy, and meticulously do everything right to not get in trouble again. Thirty years later, you are working for a guy that may have similar traits to your school teacher and—bam! You subconsciously transferred the imprint of the past experience onto your boss and now it's only a matter of time before that experience plays itself out once more. Hopefully this time you have more wisdom and can view the bigger picture. By viewing these experiences as an opportunity to have greater accountability and to stand up for yourself by not giving your personal power over to another individual, you can express gratitude for the lessons learned rather than feeling resentment for the experience. I know, it sounds too simplistic when there are emotions involved but everything comes down to your perspective on how you view your everyday life experiences. By consciously choosing to be a student in your life no matter the experience, your perception shifts and the energy that you were expending to maintain negative emotions lifts and expands your energy instead.

The next level of gratitude is to be grateful for something that hasn't happened yet. We were all conditioned as toddlers to say "thank you" when someone gave us a cookie or assisted us. This expression of gratitude came after we received what we needed and when it was socially expected to express gratitude. But, when you shift your expression of gratitude toward a desired outcome *before it occurs*, you are transmitting a vibration out into the field of creation and magnifying the possibility of what you desire coming into creation.

Why does this work? Because gratitude is not limited to the tone of your voice but rather is an emotional state of feeling satiated and complete. Although it sounds rather lovely to be able to feel gratitude for that extra money in your bank account, a new car, and a healthy body, because these are all good things and easily something to be grateful for, you might wonder, "How can I feel the emotion of gratitude for something I don't have yet, since I don't know what it feels like to have a nest egg in my bank account or a new car, and certainly, in this moment, I don't know how to access the feelings of gratitude for a healthy body?" Although you may not know what these things feel like, the joy of creating the life you desire is an important skill to develop. Visualize the life you desire in great detail and feel it in current form. Then, express gratitude much like an actress would in their acceptance speech after winning an Oscar award. Create your internal dialogue around the people that helped you to get where you are and express how your life has transformed and the joy you feel each day.

Let's take the situation of wanting a new car. To access the emotion of gratitude for a new car you haven't yet received, you will need to get crystal clear about the type of car you desire. What make and model is it? What color? What is the interior like? Visualize yourself standing in the parking lot of the dealership and shaking hands with the sales agent. Feel that excitement run through you at the pressure of a firm handshake that closes the deal. Express gratitude for the perfect car. Feel the excitement of learning all the fun gadgets on the dash. Hear the soft hum of the engine as you drive down the freeway. Where will you go in your new car? Whose lives will be enhanced because you made the choice to upgrade your lifestyle—perhaps a teenager that is excited to buy your old car? Maybe your children will now have rear air conditioning? The more clarity you can create in this visualization, the more you can tap into the vibration of gratitude for the car that you are bringing into your life.

Don't get hung up on how your desires will come forth. In matters of who, what, when, where, why, and how—how is the bottom rung of the ladder. Think of "how" as the least common denominator of creation because anyone can eventually accomplish "how" through applying consistent effort to a task, though it takes time and determination. When you keep your focus on the "why" and access the emotion of gratitude that it is already in your life, you will align yourself with that which you desire.

Let's address this from a health perspective, which adds an additional critical element into the mix: your own body. When it was the car that you felt gratitude for there wasn't a tremendous risk because most people don't need a new car to thrive in life. There are used cars that you can get by with, other people have cars that you can borrow or rent, and there is often public transportation. Not to mention that the desired car is not a living presence, actively sensing when you are sending out a vibration. The car is not sitting on the lot feeling your sabotaging thoughts about why you haven't already got the car, or your anger at the car for not arriving when you need it. But your body is a living organism that instantaneously recognizes every thought, action, and emotion that you send out and responds accordingly. This is a great reminder to continue to send love and gratitude to your body. Feel gratitude that you are still alive, for all the work your body has had to do to get you where you are today, and for your body's willingness to endure, even when your soul can't take one more minute.

Expand your gratitude toward a goal that you want to accomplish when you are healed. You may not be able to access gratitude for what it feels like to run an Ironman when you have spent the last six months in bed, but lean your emotions into the direction of that feeling. Perhaps you can begin by remembering how you played as a child, running around the soccer field. Feel gratitude for those memories and mentally work your way up to an improved gratitude state. Like attracts like. The more time you spend in the emotional state of gratitude, the easier it will be to maintain and improve. You will see your life differently and each circumstance will be viewed through a new lens.

Even though I spent months in chronic and miserable pain, I was not at a level 10 pain state every moment of every day, although admittedly, it sometimes felt that way. In the first moments of waking up I often felt normal and pain-free. I would feel a giddiness within me, thinking, "Today is the day that I am officially healed." I truly hoped and prayed that this would be true and played out in my mind all of the wonderful experiences that I was grateful to have in the coming day. This only took a few moments each morning but I did believe that it could be true and after all, that was the point. To believe that it could be true was enough to condition my mind to remember what a healthy body felt like. To hold my attention on the sensation of health when my body was showing signs of the opposite gave me a sense of hope. And, even though the symptoms would inevitably show up again, I could access gratitude for wellness and hold my attention on that emotional state as much as possible, knowing that pain would be temporary and that hope is always possible.

RESTORATIVE SLEEP

We live in a world that never sleeps. You can watch movies 24/7, restaurants deliver twenty-four hours a day, and online shopping is endless. Technology has offered up an endless array of entertainment, services, and connection with others. Our smartphones can run all night, but our bodies do not run on an external electrical current. We require rest to build up our energy supply.

To have better cognitive function, have more natural energy, and enable healing and regeneration, you need to get a full night of deep sleep. Unfortunately, it has become a social norm to try to get by with less sleep. Your body is always communicating with you, so listen to your body's signal for sleep to see if you need more. There may be a tendency to forge through the day by taking stimulants, but stimulants can create additional problems by overstimulating your adrenal glands. The greatest gift you can give yourself while you are healing is additional rest.

Your body has an internal clock known as the circadian rhythm. This sleep/wake cycle is designed to regulate your sleepiness and alertness over a twenty-four-hour time frame and is controlled by an area in the brain that responds to light. This rhythm can vary from person to person and can change as you age or when your routine changes. Ideally, though, you should attune your sleep cycle to rise with the sun and sleep when it is dark, because people in general function better this way.

Many cultures outside of the United States recognize this natural rhythm and even block out rest time between 1 and 3 p.m. Siesta anyone? While siestas are more typical in hotter climates where an afternoon nap helps restore depleted energy, plenty of mothers in the United States also take advantage of naps to catch up on sleep missed the night before. Yet as a stay-at-home mother, I rarely allowed myself to nap, even when my babies were very young. I was always afraid that someone may come to my home midday and if I were caught napping that somehow this equated to me being lazy. The few times I gave myself permission to rest, I gave myself only a few moments. Did you catch the lame belief that I had? To be honest, getting over the ridiculous idea that my rest made others view me as weak has taken me a long time. It was a deep-seated belief that held no real value and only limited my healing potential. The core belief was rooted in a lack of self-value and a belief that as a stay-at-home mother, my job was to clean, organize, and cook all day. As if to imply that because I had no paying job, I had to stay in my job twenty-four hours a day, which is often the case for a mother of young children, so the importance for rest whenever possible should be reinforced. In truth, I now admire others that respect their body's need for rest and I have finally relinquished the need to be any different. When you need rest—give yourself permission to do so.

Another component to restorative sleep is that you need it to provide the energy that will allow you to make changes in your life. How many times have you woken up inspired to change your diet, or start exercising, or reach out to someone because of an idea that came to you, only to get busy with the day, begin feeling run down again, and all bets are off? I imagine you then may have found yourself lying on the couch with a box of cookies, thinking, "I'll do it tomorrow."

Lower physical energy equals lower vibrational energy. When you are physically fatigued and worn down, Spirit is not going to give you inspiration because you need all the reserves that you have to function. Getting restorative sleep opens the door for inspiration and gives you the energy you need to take action.

It's true that we all require a different amount of nightly sleep. But if we're not getting what we need, however many hours that may be, that continued sleep deprivation can affect our health in numerous ways, bringing with it increased risk of cancer and heart disease, increased cortisol levels, higher blood pressure, insulin resistance, and weight gain. The benefits of a good night sleep include an improved immune system and a decrease in inflammation.

When you are asleep your mind releases toxins and experiences a reset, engaging the parasympathetic nervous system. The parasympathetic system is active with recovery, rest, and proper digestion. The sympathetic nervous system is your fight-or-flight system. When it is active, your body is not trying to take in valuable nutrients. Instead, it flushes out undigested food, shunting blood from your digestion to pump blood and energy to your limbs and brain. The sympathetic response, over time, suppresses your immune system and strains your adrenal glands, causing adrenal fatigue and exhaustion.

In many cultures, including in the United States, it's all about accomplishing goals and feeling overwhelmed as you try to find time for everything on your list. We live in a high-octane world but our bodies were not designed to stay in this fight-or-flight mode. We are designed to live most of our life in the parasympathetic mode. The sympathetic nervous reaction should be brief, but instead, is something many people experience as much as six hours a day. Rather than healing, recovering, and balancing our systems we are constantly tearing them down.

Once your system has been activated into the sympathetic state it often takes a great deal of time to recalibrate and relax. Sleep is the simplest way to rebalance into the parasympathetic mode. (Other helpful methods are tapping and meditation, which I cover later in this chapter.)

If a busy mental state is hindering you from getting into a deep sleep, here are a few tips to assist you:

- Take a few moments to write out any unfinished business from the day. Fear of not remembering tasks that are incomplete will hold you hostage until you can put them to rest (pun intended). This is also a good time to journal about your healing progression, or write out an emotional release in the "write and destroy" technique discussed in chapter 6 (as a refresher, this technique involves writing about a negative emotion, starting with the words, "I feel..." When you are finished you either throw the paper away, burn it, or shred it). Using this technique removes the negative emotions that were inside you and gives a sense of peace.

- Go to sleep at the same time each night and maintain a healthy sleep/wake cycle.

- Block light by adjusting the light from your clock and pulling the shades on the windows.

- Make your bedroom inviting and free of clutter. Clear off your nightstand of old magazines, mail, and pill bottles. Even when I was in bed for several weeks at a time, my husband would change the sheets each week and keep laundry off the floor. Any clutter will cause a heaviness in the room.

- Keep your room cool but not cold. Open the window for fresh air if possible.

- Avoid caffeine or stimulants in the afternoon. Start to wind down your environment in the early evening. This signals your brain that you are entering rest mode.

- Don't go to bed with your phone or laptop and don't watch television as you settle in. The blue light emitted from these devices can be stimulating.

- If your mind is racing, think of a simple word such as love, peace, calm, relax, God, rest, or still. Much like a mantra that is used during meditation, repeating a single word engages the mind intentionally rather than letting it run the show and run excessively into thoughts that are emotionally charged. Choose any word that feels good to you and internally repeat your word while engaging in slow rhythmic breathing. This will shut out distracting thoughts and quiet the mind.

- Take a supplement such as melatonin to assist you in reaching a deeper and more prolonged sleep state.

- Listen to gentle music or a meditation CD. Guided imagery for healing is a great way to support your visualization as you enter sleep.

TAPPING

There are certain healing techniques that some people won't try until everything else has failed and they finally surrender, thinking, what do I have to lose? This is often because the hype around the benefits of the technique combined with its simplicity make the whole thing seem unreal. But the benefit is often very real.

Tapping is one of those techniques. So, why does it work? Well, it has to do with cortisol. The stress hormone cortisol is a powerful player and we culturally have become cortisol junkies. Physicians know the impact of cortisol in the body and utilize it when doing an organ transplant. Before they put an organ into the recipient's body they will give that patient cortisol, or prednisone, to suppress the immune system and block the body's ability to reject the new organ. This is obviously of benefit if you are receiving a transplant but, unfortunately, in our everyday life we are doing the same thing to our body by the onslaught of continuous stress.

Your body's stress response starts in the amygdala, an almond-shaped component of the limbic system. Your amygdala is responsible for emotions such as anger, fear, grief, and sadness and controls your fight-or-flight response to stress. The amygdala is hyperactivated when your body is experiencing physical pain or when you experience stress. Your body does not distinguish between what your amygdala perceives as a threat versus the constant barrage of stress in today's lifestyle, so whether it was triggered by a real physical threat or financial worries, your amygdala sends out the troops to help you battle a physical threat.

Throughout human history there has always been some level of stress, such as accessing your next meal or running from the proverbial tiger. In today's world, we watch media footage of war-torn countries while the news crawl at the bottom of the screen gives accounts of child abduction or a gang-related murder. Our circle of friends has expanded to a global level and we are the fly on the wall to everything other people get to enjoy via social media, reminding us of what we are missing out on. Our children are overscheduled, always trying to stay above average and increase their potential for success, which adds to our already full schedule. This all leads to chronic stress.

Your amygdala senses these incoming stress points as danger and prompts your body to release adrenaline and the stress hormone cortisol. This fight-or-flight response is designed to protect you from an immediate and brief threat by shutting down healing and digestion and redirecting valuable energy to your brain and muscles. Your blood pressure and heartbeat rises and your senses become more acute—all to give you the edge for survival. Remember, your body and brain behave equally to a perceived threat or an actual threat. Over time, this continued stress on the body causes a cascade of problems, including heart disease, digestive issues, obesity, migraines, depression, and a lowered immune response. Tapping breaks the association between stress and the amygdala.

Tapping, also known as EFT (Emotional Freedom Technique), uses the body's meridian points as a form of physical and emotional healing. It is based on the same energy meridians that have been used in traditional acupuncture to treat physical and emotional ailments for thousands of years, but works without the invasive use of needles.

Meridians are the energy channels that carry your vital force energy and connect to the organs and other systems throughout your body. Every meridian has an endpoint that is located on the surface of your body where you can access these energy channels. These endpoints are commonly used in acupuncture treatments to balance the various body systems. Tapping on the specific meridians while addressing an emotional or physical stress sends a calming response to the body and allows the amygdala to turn off the stress response. Using tapping in conjunction with thinking or speaking aloud about the issue retrains the limbic system by signaling the amygdala that all is well and deactivates the stress response. This technique can be used for stress, release of physical pain, trauma, and PTSD. While tapping is not a cure for disease or illness, it is an incredibly powerful tool to support releasing negative emotions and stress that are stored in the body.

By tapping the tips of your fingers on these various points and focusing your attention on a specific emotional or physical stress, you release the emotional charge surrounding the issue or concern. Emotions and physical sensations are your body's way of communicating. Tapping assists you in overcoming negative beliefs, pain, and emotions that are held in the body and addresses the mind-body connection by rewiring the brain.

The channels of energy in the body can get blocked by emotional or physical trauma. Tapping on the various endpoints provides an energetic disruption to these emotional and physical traumas by signaling the amygdala to halt the fight-or-flight response. The primary tapping sequence involves nine meridian endpoints and is designed to address all the major endpoints throughout the mind and body. While a person is tapping, they are releasing healing hormones and activating the body's self-repair mechanisms. During a tapping session, you would tap on the sequence of end points while you focus your attention on the pain, anxiety, limiting belief, fear, or stress that you want to resolve.

I know what you are thinking at this point. "Wait? What? Those all sound negative. Why would I hold my attention on the negative when it's those thoughts that got me where I am in the first place? Doesn't focusing on pain and fear just create more of what I don't want?" The simple answer is no. The reality is that these negative thoughts are already present at some level within you whether you think and talk about them consciously or not. For this technique, it is important to momentarily acknowledge the physical or emotional pain to highlight what you are removing. Ignoring what exists doesn't mean that it isn't there.

Imagine having a room in your basement that you use to store everything that you no longer need but haven't gotten rid of yet: old magazines, outdated clothes, broken appliances and worn-out furniture. You keep the door closed in case company comes over so nobody sees what is inside of that room. Over time you continue to increase the clutter, causing it to spill over into other rooms. If you envision your body much like this storage room of unprocessed chaos you'll see that the tapping sequence is simply acknowledging what is already there and by holding your attention on it you are opening the door, turning on the light, and clearing it out.

The concern that most people have when they are first introduced to tapping is the fear that they are "doing it wrong." I know this was a concern for me and I realized that I got hung up on the details rather than just allowing the process.

I encourage you to not get hung up on making sure that you use the right words. You will find that the language you use is not the most important factor. Rather, it's tapping on the meridian points while you hold your attention on the negativity that you are clearing.

Listed below are the simple steps in a tapping session:

1. Choose an emotional or physical issue that you want to address. Tapping on a meridian point sends a response to the body. You will want to direct the tapping experience by choosing a specific concern to address. This can be anything that you want to resolve—physical pain, limiting beliefs, trauma from your past, or unresolved emotional disturbances. Take a moment and think of what has been your biggest current obstacle and try to get as specific as possible. Do you want to release fear? Let go of emotional trauma? Experience pain relief? Let go of limiting beliefs? We all have multiple issues that we could address but during a tapping sequence it is important that you choose to focus on one at a time. Be as specific and clear as possible. If I were to ask you, "What is the biggest hurdle in your life right now?" What would your answer be? Possible answers could be:

I have horrible joint pain.

I feel overwhelmed with my responsibilities.

I feel frustrated at my body for not healing.

I feel afraid that I might die.

I'm scared about my upcoming surgery.

Use your intuition to come up with a concern that you want to address. Don't worry; you can't get this wrong. If you have several issues that come up, pick one to start with. Try to be as specific as you can. Rather than just tapping and thinking, "my body hurts," think of what specific ways and areas that your body hurts, such as "the inflammation in my joints hurts." The more specific you are in addressing the issue the better you are able to focus more clearly on the concern you would like to release. Don't worry about using the perfect language—the most important element is to focus on the emotion. It's important to remember that it's not the circumstance, person, or the physical sensations that are causing distress but rather how you feel about them that is causing you emotional disturbances. It may also benefit you to visualize a specific event that you would like to release.

2. Decide on a reminder phrase. Your reminder phrase is your primary concern or issue, simplified down to just a few words that you will use throughout the tapping sequence. For example, if your issue or concern is frustration at your body for not healing, while you are tapping you would say out loud, "This frustration... This frustration... This frustration..." In the example below, the reminder phrase is "This pain... This pain... This pain..." The point of repeating your reminder phrase is to keep your focus on the issue that you are addressing rather than allowing your mind to wander. Your reminder phrase is also a guiding tool that helps you to unearth emotions that may be coming up in relation to the original issue. When you become comfortable in performing the tapping sequence you can adjust the reminder phrase at each of the various points if you desire. For example, at one point you might say, "This frustration that I am feeling..." Then at others you might say, "I feel so much frustration with my body... All of this frustration... I feel frustrated that I don't have control over my body..."

3. Rate the intensity of your problem on a scale of 0 to 10. Once you are clear on the issue that you want to address and have created a reminder phrase, decide on the level of intensity you feel regarding your issue. A level 10 would be the most extreme intensity you can imagine; 0 would mean that you would feel no concern at all. Again, use your intuition. I suggest that you start with an issue that you rate at least a 6 or higher to notice a significant shift in the issue from the technique. It's important to measure your intensity before you begin as an indicator of improvement. Otherwise, you may not remember how you originally felt about something before releasing some of the emotional intensity and so you may not recognize that you have released anything. By choosing to rate your intensity level before you begin, then rechecking the intensity level after your tapping sequence, you can gauge whether you have had improvement.

4. Create a setup statement. It is important to create a setup statement to bring forward and fully activate the issue that you want to address. Typically, a setup statement will go something like this: *Even though* _____ (fill in the blank with the issue you are addressing), *I deeply and completely love and accept myself.* So, continuing with the original issue of frustration with your body your setup statement might be, "Even though I feel frustrated with my body, I deeply and completely love and accept myself."

Before we move on I would like to address the statement, "I deeply and completely love and accept myself." This may be challenging for you to say if what you're feeling about yourself is not love and acceptance, but rather anger and intolerance. I encourage you to use these words anyway. You may not feel that you love and accept yourself in your current state, but self-acceptance is a valuable component to healing. By giving yourself permission to love and accept who you are right now you have the potential to uproot and release layers of emotional pain that you haven't looked at before. Once you have your setup statement, you can begin the tapping process.

5. Tap on the karate chop point while repeating your setup statement three times (refer to the diagram further in this section to identify the points). After this, you will move on to tap through the other eight points of the tapping sequence.

6. Tap through the eight points in the EFT sequence while repeating your reminder phrase out loud. You can tap on either the left or right side, or both sides at the same time since the same meridians run down both sides of the body. Tap on whichever side feels most comfortable for you. Using the tips of your fingers, tap at each point at least five times in a row before moving on to the next point. As you work through the tapping sequence, continue to repeat your reminder phrase. You can tap each point as many times as feels comfortable, but it's typical to tap between five and ten times.

7. After each round of the tapping sequence, take a deep breath. Again, rate the intensity of your issue using the 0 to 10 scale of intensity to identify your progress. Tune into your body and feel if there has been a shift. Was there a decrease in intensity? What other thoughts, emotions, sensations, or memories came up? The real magic happens when you go deeper.

8. Repeat the process in steps 5 through 7 until you feel good about the progress you made. Many times, there is a profound, lasting shift that takes place in a single tapping experience. If this happens for you, awesome! But there can also be times when symptoms or emotions initially feel more intense rather than better. This is often because of the multiple layers of emotions you are releasing, or because you may have had unrelated thoughts or emotions surface that were triggered during the tapping sequence. Be patient with yourself and keep tapping. The thing to remember about tapping, and well, pretty much everything else in this book, is in order for you to get the benefits that tapping can offer, it is imperative that you just do it.

The following is a suggested script for stress and anxiety. You can adjust the language to make it more specific to you. As you go through the different tapping points, say the statement out loud.

You may notice that the tapping script is focused on emotions rather than behavior. Our behaviors are fueled by emotion—at times stress and anxiety can be quite debilitating. When we resolve the emotional distress, our behavior shifts. The possibilities really are tremendous.

The meridian points for the EFT sequence are in the following order. You will begin with three rounds at the **Karate Chop (KC)** point, then continue the sequence by tapping the following points:

Eyebrow (EB): On the inside edge of the eyebrow just above the bridge of the nose.

Side of Eye (SE): On the side of the outer edge of either eye.

Under Eye (UE): On the bone below the center of the eye.

Under Nose (UN): On the philtrum between the nose and the upper lip.

Chin (CH): Midpoint between the mouth and chin.

Collarbone (CB): Between the sternum and collarbone, about one inch left or right from the center of the body.

Under Arm (UA): Under the arm at the area of a woman's bra, about four inches below the armpit.

Top of Head (TH): On the crown of the head.

See Tapping Point Reference Guide on next page.

Tapping Point Reference Guide

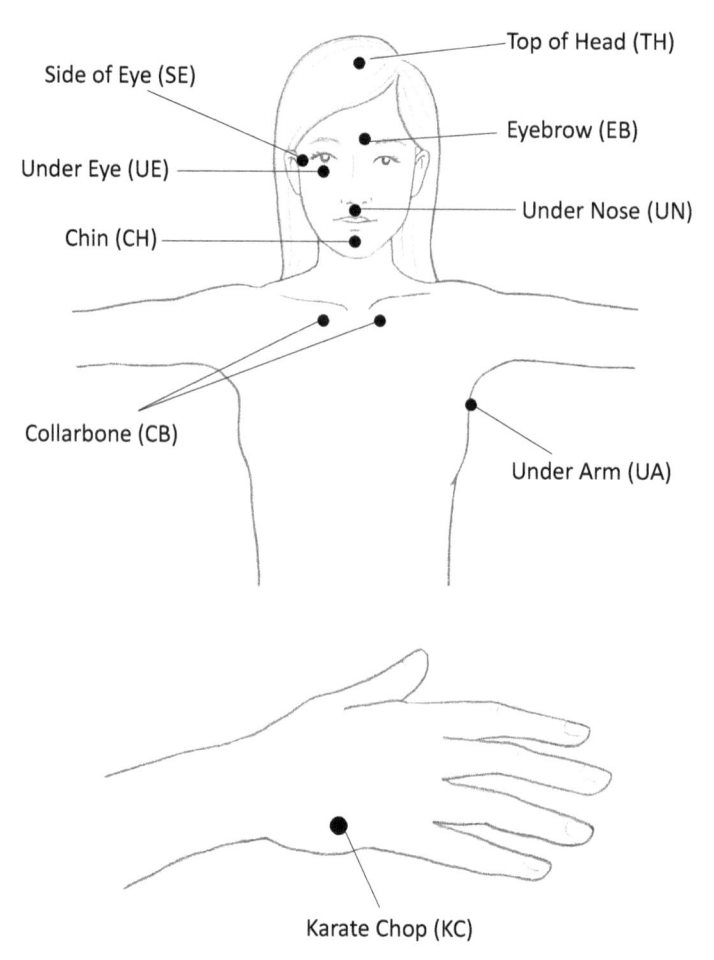

- Top of Head (TH)
- Side of Eye (SE)
- Eyebrow (EB)
- Under Eye (UE)
- Under Nose (UN)
- Chin (CH)
- Collarbone (CB)
- Under Arm (UA)
- Karate Chop (KC)

Before you begin tapping, ask yourself, "What is causing me to feel pain in my body? Where is this pain located? What are recurring symptoms that I can't seem to get over?" It is helpful if you can get to the root of the emotions by identifying a primary event or concern that caused you to have a stress response in regards to the pain. Was it a doctor visit where a lump was found? A trip to the emergency room? A car accident or surgery that you didn't fully recover from? As a means of support in identifying the emotional response, it may be helpful to assign your pain an image. Then ask yourself why you chose that image. Was it sharp because it feels intense or angry? Was it cloudy because there is a feeling of hopelessness? Or large because your emotions feel bigger than you?

Tune into your body and notice any areas where you hold stress because of pain. Notice any shortness of breath; tightness in your shoulders, chest, or neck; headache; or distress in your abdomen. These are all signs of an imbalance in the body.

Before you begin with the script, remember to first rate your pain intensity on a scale of 0 to 10. While working through the sequence along with the script, personalize it by identifying your specific pain, replacing the general "in my body" with more specific phrases like "in my stomach" or "in my right breast." The more specific you are, the more your brain can unravel the hardwiring that is associated with the issue.

Tapping Script for Pain

Begin by tapping on the Karate Chop point then continue to move through the various tapping points while repeating the statements below. Feel free to adjust the language to fit your needs.

KC: Even though I have this pain in my body, I deeply and completely love and accept myself.

KC: Even though this pain is wearing me down and my body aches from all this pressure that I feel, I deeply and completely love and accept myself.

KC: Even though on an unconscious level I'm frozen with fear because of the pain I am feeling, I deeply and completely love and accept myself as I am.

EB: All this pain that I am feeling.

SE: I am feeling so much pain that it scares me.

UE: My nervous system feels raw with stress because of this pain.

UN: I can feel my body ache with all the fear of the unknown.

CH: I don't feel safe in my body and it's just too much.

CB: I feel powerless to control the pain that I feel.

UA: I feel fear because I don't have control over the pain that I feel.

TH: I feel afraid of all this pain; it's just too much for me.

EB: All this pain that I am feeling.

SE: So much pain in my body.

UE: This pain has been with me so long I don't remember not feeling this way.

UN: All this pain in my body makes me want to give up.

CH: I feel afraid that I am never going to recover.

CB: I don't know how to let go of all this pain.

UA: I choose to let go and release all of this pain from my body.

TH: I am open to the possibility of a better way and living pain-free.

Take a deep breath and check in with how your body feels. Notice if there were any physical or emotional shifts. Rate your level of intensity on the scale of 0 to 10. Did the intensity go down? If so, great. If not, stay with it and do a few more rounds. It may be beneficial to continue through the tapping points and do a narrative of a specific experience that is causing you to feel distress with the pain. Were there any other emotions or thoughts that surfaced during the tapping session? If so, look at those as an opportunity to go deeper with the healing process.

When you are ready and have released most of the negative intensity, you can tap on positive attributes you would like to integrate more into your life. You don't want to force the positive to show up but rather allow it to come into being once you have released some level of negative intensity. If you notice some mental chatter during a positive tapping session, expressing resistance or a feeling that what you're saying is not true, you may wish to go back to clearing out the negative emotions until you arrive at a more neutral space.

Positive Tapping Script

Check into your body and notice any sensations. Take a few deep breaths and begin tapping on the points.

KC: Even though I have symptoms of pain in my body, I am open to releasing them now.

KC: Even though there is so much pressure that I feel internally, I trust that there is a better way for me.

KC: Even though I can't remember a time when I was free of pain, I allow the possibility for this to arrive in my life.

EB: I recognize that I use these patterns of pain to make me feel safe.

SE: I have found a better way that is supportive and kind to my body.

UE: I release the pain I have been holding onto. I remember what it feels like to feel good.

UN: I allow my body to relax as I release the pain from my body.

CH: I allow the feeling of peace to wash over me.

CB: My body is feeling calmer and more relaxed as I release the pain that I have held onto.

UA: I am ready to feel whole and at peace with who I am.

TH: This peace is infusing my body with love.

EB: I have greater control over how I respond to my environment.

SE: Regardless of the stress in my life, I choose to feel peace.

UE: I take back my power and I choose to feel peace right now.

UN: All of this peace I am feeling in my body.

CH: It feels good to be relaxed and calm.

CB: I trust in the divine to support me in my life.

UA: I trust in the divine to support me with my body.

TH: I trust in the divine that all is well.

As with the previous script, if you don't get results right away, continue to tap and be patient with yourself. And continue to check in with your body and go through the tapping sequence when new emotions appear.

MEDITATION

Meditation is a technique you have probably heard about but not necessarily taken the time to implement. I used to think that if I were ever forced to be in bed because of an illness I would use that time wisely and meditate, because then I would finally have the time to do it. I knew multiple techniques of meditation, since I was formally trained in Transcendental Meditation in 1991, and Vipassana Meditation in 2006. However, I resisted implementing a regular meditation discipline until just a few years ago. My early approach to meditation was that it was another task to accomplish in my already overbooked daily schedule rather than an opportunity to quiet my mind and gain the stillness that my body needed.

Although many people have been told they should incorporate meditation for their health or to reduce stress, the thought of sitting and doing nothing seems extremely counterproductive when there are so many things to get done. Right? You may have agreed to give it a shot when the stress in your life felt overwhelming. Anyone that has done so can attest it pretty much goes as follows: You sit down, cross your legs, uncomfortably resting each foot on the opposite thigh. You place your hands in your lap, close your eyes, and take a few breaths. It takes a few minutes to adjust your body but you are determined to get this right. You've kept your eyes closed for what seems like twenty minutes, and you look at the clock to see that only two minutes have passed. Ugh! Meditation is so hard... But, you are determined to give it another go and forty-five seconds later, you open your eyes again to conclude that your clock is clearly broken because it hasn't moved and you have been sitting for what feels like an eternity.

You eventually decide you must be doing it wrong because nothing happened. Your mind wandered to your to-do list and, truth be told, it was boring. You quickly ascertain you are wasting valuable time and now, have less time to accomplish what needs to get done.

Meditation is a time of self-reflection and renewal. By quieting the mind you enter a state of receiving greater awareness. Sitting down to "try" to meditate misses the point all together and is similar to trying to go to sleep. The more effort you engage in the trying, the more resistance you feel. In the act of trying, you continue the cycle of doing rather than being. By releasing effort and softening the rhythm of your breath, you drop into the state of being in awareness. This is where the magic happens in meditation.

From the first moments upon waking most of us engage in an endless chain of thoughts. One after another. This can cause us to disengage from the present moment into thoughts of the past or projections into the future. The purpose of meditation is to calm the mind and to enter the space between thought. It is in this void where inspiration and healing comes in.

Mindfulness Meditation is derived from the Buddhist practice known as Vipassana. It is a form of meditation designed to develop awareness and to remain equanimous. Being equanimous is a state of mind where you are not striving for or resisting whatever comes up in your thoughts or physical sensations; by staying neutral you allow thoughts to flow through while simply observing them. In observation, you are not trying to grasp the thought as a craving to hold onto and not running away in resistance. Instead, you are allowing yourself to just be and accepting what is. This invites the awareness that you are not your thoughts but rather an observer of thought, which can potentially reduce old thought patterns or attachments to negative feelings.

When you sit down to meditate, your mind will grab at your attention by remembering things to get done and inspire the urge to act on them. This is part of the process. When those thoughts come in, and they will, simply redirect your attention back to your breath.

It is important to have a point of focus when beginning a meditation practice. In Vipassana meditation the focus of awareness is with the breath, which serves as an anchor to the present moment.

Initially, the idea of being present in the moment can be frightening at times, especially for someone that is experiencing physical pain. And during meditation, it can be common for a specific part of your body to be screaming for attention via physical pain. This causes your brain to sound the blow horn, screaming "fix me!" Obviously, it's responsible to follow up with the needs of your physical body but remember that even when you are doing all that you can, healing takes time. By being fully present and aware, you calm your mind away from what hurts and remove the constant attention from the problem, which otherwise, can deepen you into a state of despair and frustration.

It can also be hard to be present because we live in a world of time pressure and overscheduled agendas and have lost the ability to be fully present in the moment. For many years, I believed I was present and just happened to be a great multitasker. I would fix dinner while catching up on a favorite show on TV, during the same time that I would be catching up with my children about their day at school. I believed I was maximizing my point of contact with the world around me but in fact, many times, I was so lost in a loop of thought that I wasn't present at all, often asking my children to repeat what they told me because I missed it completely. We've all done it, but that doesn't mean it's a good idea. Our brains don't have the ability to focus on multiple things at once. For someone that understands the value of awareness and finds themselves in this cycle, they could simply redirect their attention to a singular engagement and focus on their breath to become more present.

Transcendental Meditation, also called TM, is a practice that is taught by a certified teacher. This practice has a tremendous amount of research supporting its benefits, but official training can be quite costly for someone that is on a limited budget. The intention is that with proper instruction one can transcend the busy and often agitated mind, arriving, momentarily, to no thought and no sound, in the space of stillness. In the training the teacher will provide the student a mantra that is personalized to deepen their meditation practice.

A mantra is a word or sound that is repeated silently as a means of strengthening your mind. Initially, a mantra will compete with the thoughts you are having. By focusing your attention on the mantra, you condition your mind to realize that it is not in control. When your mind shifts back into thought, which it will do repeatedly, simply redirect your attention by repeating your mantra.

Some people may feel concerned that a meditation practice will conflict with their religious views. Meditation is not a religion, but it can support any religious practice. One of my favorite psalms is Psalm 46:10, "Be still and know that I am God." It is in the stillness of meditation and prayer that we open the pathways to receiving spiritual guidance. You can think of prayer and meditation as two supportive natures of the same connective force. In prayer, you are asking your higher power for grace, guidance, and messages of inspiration. In meditation, you are the receiver of such.

Meditation is a practice that can have great benefits at any age, is free, and can take as little as two minutes a day to have a valuable impact. So why are more people not implementing meditation into their lives? Fear is a large inhibitor when it comes to trying something new. You may have questioned, "What if I do it wrong?" Or, "What if I'm not good at it?" Take the fear out of meditation by familiarizing yourself with the basic goals of a regular meditation practice and realize that practice is just that—practice. No one does it one hundred percent right all the time.

Another reason many people don't implement meditation is a feeling of not having enough time. My favorite quote in regards to this concern is a Zen proverb that says, "Every person should meditate for twenty minutes every day. For those that don't have time to meditate—they need an hour." This is because when you are burdened down with responsibility and running your life like a drill sergeant, you remove yourself from life's natural flow and create chaos around you. Think of the times when you were rushing out the door and ended up taking more time than expected because of the coffee you spilled on your shirt, tripping over the shoes left by the door. Think of how you hit your elbow against the door jam and left your cell phone on the counter, having to return home to grab it. These are all signs to slow down and get back in rhythm. Meditation provides this rebalancing.

Meditation quiets the constant scattered thinking that often brings anxiety, worry, and distraction, and brings you back into the present moment. Meditation has been shown to ease depression, lower blood pressure, improve mental function, and reduce stress and anxiety. Meditation can increase theta brain wave activity, calming the amygdala, allowing your nervous system to enter the parasympathetic state necessary for healing.

To support your meditation practice, I have listed a few keys to success below.

Keys to Successful Meditation

1. Set your intention and stick to it. Having clear objectives (how many times a day, what time of day, and for how long) will give you the determination you need to be successful.

2. Create your own meditation sanctuary. This could be your closet, a corner in your bedroom, or office. Add some soft cushions, candles, or music—anything that gives you a sense of peace and conditions your mind to view this space and time as sacred.

3. Tune the external world out and turn your attention inward. Turn off your phone and notify family members that this is your meditation time so that you will not be interrupted.

4. Don't decide to meditate based upon your mood or energy. Emotions and energy change throughout the day, every day. Meditate anyway.

5. Ideally, find a comfortable chair to support you in sitting upright. This aligns your body with the proper flow of energy

and conditions your body to enter a meditative space. Your mind associates your bed with sleep, so I don't recommend meditating there if you have the option to sit up elsewhere. There is still benefit for those who are bedridden, though. Adjust your practice to your individual needs.

6. Rather than looking at meditation as another task or a chore that needs to get done, approach your meditation as a chance to surrender and release resistance by putting the mind-body into a simple being state. Thinking of it as something to mark off your to-do list causes you to go into a doing mode.

7. Prepare your body before you begin. It's often helpful to do a few yoga stretches or slow deep breathing for two to five minutes before you sit down to meditate. This will help to burn off any residual energy or restlessness and allows your mind to become centered in a more peaceful state.

8. As you make yourself comfortable, relax your face with a soft smile. This releases feel-good hormones and a sense that all is well.

9. Don't use this time to visualize and create. Doing so activates the mind. Instead, meditate first and relax your mind into the theta brain wave state. As you may recall, this is the state of imagination and creation. Once you have accessed this brain state through meditation, you can follow your mediation with visualization exercises, which you will likely move through with greater ease and success.

10. Use tools such as sounds in nature, music, incense, candles, or guided imagery audio CDs to support your meditation practice.

11. Recognize that each meditation experience will be different. Don't set the goal to remain in a blissful state the entire time. See success in simply acknowledging that bliss can be achievable, if even for a moment.

The following are four variations of a meditation exercise. Try to work up to a meditation practice of fifteen to twenty minutes, twice a day.

One ideal time to meditate is in the morning, upon arising, when the bridge between the conscious state and subconscious is still open in the first fifteen to twenty minutes of waking. This will energize you for the day. A deep state of meditation can relax the mind more deeply than some sleep states, so doing this in the morning can also help you feel more well rested—which may be especially important if you have been experiencing pain that disrupts your sleep. The other optimal times of day to meditate are in the late afternoon, before your evening meal, or before bed. Be aware that if you schedule your meditation time before bed, you may find yourself too fatigued and bypass your meditation practice, whereas if you schedule it before dinner, you still allow for family time in the evening and creating a ritual for sleep.

Twenty minutes can feel like a long time when you first begin, and a sense of having to slog through your practice can halt the desire to pursue it more. So start slowly with two to three minutes at a time and work your way up. Before you begin, you should loosen your belt and remove your shoes, jewelry, watch, and glasses, to limit any restrictions or sensations that could be distracting. Sit comfortably and close your eyes. Take a few deep cleansing breaths and then continue with one of the suggested techniques below. In all of the following meditations, when you get distracted by physical sensations, thoughts, or sounds, simply return your attention back to either your mantra or your breath.

Mantra meditation: As noted earlier, a mantra is a chosen sound or word that is repeated silently as a way of focusing your mind. There are numerous mantras that originate from the Sanskrit language. Two that I prefer to use are "So-Hum," which translates as "I Am That" and helps us connect with all that is, and "Aham Prema" (pronounced pray-ma), which translates as "I Am Divine Love." These Sanskrit mantras have a high vibrational frequency to expand awareness, but you can choose any word that resonates for you. Other words that carry a high vibration include "Love," "Peace," and "Joy."

Once you have your chosen mantra, sit quietly for a few breaths, then silently begin repeating it. You may notice that your focus on your mantra will drop off and your mind will begin to wander back into thought. Do not try to silence the thoughts. In doing so you are thinking, "I must stop these thoughts," which is, in and of itself, another thought. Instead, catch yourself having thoughts, and in that awareness, simply bring your attention back to your chosen mantra. Continue throughout your practice and in the end, simply release your mantra. Stay seated for an additional few moments, then slowly open your eyes.

Breathing Meditation: It is important to note that by holding your attention on the breath that this does not mean to "think about" the breath. It is more of a "being with" the breath, by observing it rather than trying to manipulate it. In the very nature of this observation you will enter a more relaxed state, gradually deepening and slowing down the rhythm of your breathing. In this practice, sit comfortably with your eyes closed. Take a few slow breaths. Draw your attention to the nostrils and observe the sensation of breath as you inhale and exhale. Notice if the breath is moving through either the left or right nostril, or both. After a few moments, expand your awareness to the breath as it circulates throughout your system, expanding and releasing in the diaphragm and lungs. Observe thoughts as they pass through your mind with no attachments and continue to bring your attention back to the flow and rhythm of the breath. When you have completed your meditation, take a final deep cleansing breath and exhale fully. Gently open your eyes and sit peacefully for a few moments.

Mindful Self-Love Meditation: In this meditation, you will focus your attention to infuse love and light energy throughout your entire body. Years of neglect or negative emotions are detrimental to the healing process. By focusing love with intention, you release negative perceptions you may have held toward your body and begin valuing the life your body is providing for you.

You can either sit or lie down for this meditation, and close your eyes. Begin by taking a few slow, rhythmic breaths to relax your body, focusing your attention on your breath. Then move your attention up to the crown of your head and visualize a stream of beautiful white and pink light pouring through the top of your head to every cell in your body. Work your way down one side of your body to the toes and then continue to visualize this energy infusing you as you work your way back to the crown of your head. You can also do this by visualizing going down the front of your body and then returning up the back side. Visually, imagine this beautiful light healing every cell. Feel gratitude and love for every freckle, stretch mark, scar, or perceived imperfection. Shower your body with love until it is as natural as breathing. When you arrive at a specific area of your body that is diseased, in physical pain, scarred from surgery, or weak in some way, notice any emotions that come up. Again, don't avoid them—just be an observer. In these areas of the body, you can enhance your healing visualization by holding that area gently. Have compassion for the struggle that part of your body has endured. Maybe you have said negative comments to this area, or held anger or resentment toward it. Choose to release anything that is negative and continue to send loving energy. Ensure that you don't avoid any area of your body and once you have completed the process, sit still for a few more moments in gratitude for your life and for your beautiful body that is providing you with a vehicle to experience your life.

Spiritual Guidance Meditation: Spirit is always in communication with us, but it can be challenging to listen to inner guidance when you're battling illness. Unless you are comfortable listening to your own inner guidance you may feel conflicted in your ability to receive messages from spirit. Practice listening to the messages that your body is sending you. Since spiritual communication speaks in the quiet space, or void between thoughts, begin by closing your eyes and taking a few deep breaths to enter a meditative state. Go within and ask, "Where in my life am I out of balance?" As we've discussed before, illness is always an indicator that there is imbalance somewhere in your life. Ask, "What is the next step that I need to take toward my healing?" Healing in any form begins at the cellular level, within. Therefore, all answers to your healing must begin there as well. Anything from the external world is a support tool to assist you in accessing this healing.

Trust the messages that you receive but don't try to force them to come. Resist the urge to think and search for the answer. Instead, ask the question and enter a space of stillness to allow Spirit to answer. Be patient and remain in a peaceful state. Spirit does not respond in urgency or fear. If you notice either of these sensations come up, simply ask them to go away, and refocus on your breath. Allow for divine timing to provide the appropriate answers in time.

Choose to be gentle with yourself as you develop a meditation practice and keep your thoughts in a peaceful state. This is not an experience of conquer and achieve. Meditation is an act of stillness and connection with the flow of life. Whether you implement one of these meditations or use a guided imagery meditation audio, it is valuable to keep your practice alive. Think of meditation as you would eating each day. Make time to provide this nourishment to the soul by going within.

PRAYER

The act of prayer is associated with stillness and quiet reflection, turning inward and away from outer world distractions, connecting with the source of creation. There is a spectrum of religious beliefs associated with prayer, with some believing prayer should include asking forgiveness for sins and a plea for salvation. Although there are those who discourage praying for material things, many of us can testify to throwing that in there too, for good measure.

A relationship with the divine is personal, for there is no one that supersedes your direct line to this source. I respect that this is a touchy subject for some who believe that they can only communicate with God by going through the proper channels of their religious clergy but to enhance your relationship with God, you must connect one-on-one.

To have this connection, it is valuable to recognize any barriers you may have put between you and God, and yes, they are your barriers because God did not put them there. In unraveling your beliefs, you need to ask yourself, "What is keeping me from having a relationship with the divine?" Another way to look at this is by asking yourself, "If God knocked on my door, what would prevent me from answering?" Listen to your intuition and notice any emotions or beliefs rising to the surface. Is there a sense of unworthiness? Fear of judgement? Unresolved guilt for past experiences or behaviors? Anger or resentment for enduring challenges? Or perhaps, you haven't had a relationship with God before now, and thus don't see it valuable to implement. Maybe the word "God" doesn't resonate with you. That's okay—adjust the language to fit within your framework for understanding the source of all things. Creator, Heavenly Father, Divine Source, Infinite Spirit, Lord, Supreme Being, and Higher Power are a few options. Whatever word you use is completely up to you. There are many names for God and depending on your religious background, many forms of God as well. In Christianity, there is the belief in a single God that made man in the likeness of himself, whereas in Hinduism there is a belief in many gods. I respect each person's individual belief in their higher force, and honor each person's route in connecting to that nature.

I find it valuable to take an honest assessment of where your beliefs are in your relationship with a higher power. In many religions, there is a conditioning of polarity. Good versus evil and heaven versus hell. This paradigm often has the perception of God as the utilitarian father figure whose love is conditional based upon our acts of good deeds. There is an assumption that this thinking keeps us in check and provides a narrow path to walk in life due to our human weaknesses and inadequacies. However, here lies the problem with this belief. You will never measure up because you will always view yourself as a lesser being, unworthy of love lest you spend every moment of your life in a perfected state, and this is impossible. But if you can allow for an expansion in your perception of your relationship with God, and yes, it is your perception, then you can access the true power in prayer. In this relationship with God/Higher Power/Divine Source, you are co-creating every second you are awake. As a co-creator, you believe that there are an infinite number of possibilities in life; you just need to decide which possibility you would like to make manifest and turn your attention toward this desire with the knowledge of support from this source of creation. Recognize that the divine is deeply seated within your every thought and action as a guide to your spiritual advancement.

Whether you believe that God is in all things or that God is only available to a chosen few is yours to decide. My purpose for including prayer is not to adjust someone's religious or spiritual beliefs, but to enhance and deepen your connection to the great cosmos. To do so, there are two specific elements that must be present. Faith and Love.

You may have heard the statement, "Faith and fear cannot reside in the same room." In my life, I have swung far along the pendulum between faith and fear. I have prayed for answers that didn't appear and pleaded to be recognized in my desperation. I have also experienced moments of rage and anger, believing I was being punished by God. At the deepest level, I feared that God did not love me enough to "fix me" in my demands for healing. I held God accountable for all my struggle. I experienced bouts of fear that were debilitating, where my need to have control over the circumstances around me caused rigid thinking rather than trusting that nature was working out the details for my highest good. As you enter the sacredness of prayer, you need to have faith and surrender to the highest good for all concerned.

Some people claim that they can maintain a prayerful resonance within and around them throughout their day while others kneel and bow as an act of humbleness and submission to the divine. Some people consider prayer only when there doesn't seem to be any other answer for their challenges, while others try to beat challenges to the punch by showing servitude and commitment to God. As if in a silent agreement of "I bow and give praise to you and in turn, you protect me from the evils of the world."

Whether you pray in a holy temple or out in nature, the power of prayer is extraordinary and yet, something that we barely understand. There are people that mechanically recite prayer, learned by rote, as if the words themselves would be enough to grab the attention of God. Others change their daily prayer to fit their present needs and those of the people around them. In relation to prayer, there are as many ways to pray as there are people who are praying. However or wherever one enters into prayer, within the soul is always a desire to connect with the divine.

According to Dr. Larry Dossey, author of *Healing Words*, the benefits of prayer are not increased by the number of people saying the prayer, but rather the intensity and genuine focus of love. Dr. Dossey reports that multiple double- and triple-blind studies on praying indicate significant improvement on the groups that were prayed for; even though the people that were praying had no idea who they were praying for and were sometimes thousands of miles away. He continues in saying, "Prayer is as effective from opposite ends of the Earth as kneeling at the bedside of those they are praying for."

I trust that every prayer is heard and answered. But only answered to the level that we, as humans, can accept. There is not a scale based on worthiness for receiving what we are praying for—all things are energy and we simply need to be an energetic or vibrational match to receive something. And if you are reciting a prayer without connecting your heart and mind to God, how can you possibly receive the message that God is sending back to you?

I spent many years searching for the "rules" of prayer, believing that if I learned the secret code, I could bypass struggle and finally get the answers I was searching for. Again and again, I would be reminded of the value in focused thought, word, and emotion. By holding your attention on the divine, you quiet your mind and make space for the messages from God to be received, but it takes the emotion of love and being in harmony with the divine source to create this connection. In connecting your energy with the divine and aligning body, mind, and soul, you open a direct line to the sacredness of prayer.

Each of us can connect to the creative force and, through prayer, not only ask for what we desire but receive as well. The more time spent in this sacred communion, the more we become free of fear. Trust that God loves you unconditionally. Trust that your purpose on this planet is to be fulfilled as you expand your consciousness and trust that you are worthy of God's love.

The moment you put your attention toward that creative force, your soul signature is instantly seen by the great cosmic energy and your desires are in a state of creation. The great cosmic joke is that when we release our focus from how and when, these creations show up. In this, is the surrender.

Kneeling and bowing our heads is the act of surrender to the will of God. When you "let go and let God" you allow the divine force to move through you for the highest good of all.

The power of God's energy does not act independent of you but rather awakens what was already within you for your highest good by affirming in your consciousness that which already exists— a whole and complete life filled with joy, that is free of illness and disease.

I have a friend that measures the vibrational frequency of everything in his life by using kinesiology. Literally everything. He measures the frequency of the fruit in the bins at the grocery store, the vitamins on the shelf, various words, the clothes that we wear, and the people he interacts with. He also measured different forms of prayer and formulated a simple, yet elegant prayer that he has tested to have a very high vibration. It goes as follows: "God, please fill me with your unconditional love." He suggests that after saying this, you take at least sixty seconds to receive the blessings, holding your attention while saying, "I am receiving the blessings." He then recommends saying "Amen" after the minute has passed. He explains when you say "Amen," the flow of receiving the blessings is complete. Amen is your way of saying thank you. It is done.

ESSENTIAL OILS

Essential oils have been used for centuries in everything from beauty treatments to religious ceremonies. Having gained more attention in the last fifteen years, essential oils are now more mainstream and available for everyday use. With improved quality and safety standards, essential oils are finding their way into many homes around the world, replacing everything from perfume to pain relievers.

Essential oils and plant extracts are the most powerful part of the plant and their medicinal use to support the immune system and maintain health has been documented throughout history. Known for their mood-uplifting qualities, they also provide a wide range of benefits for many uses, including soothing skin irritation, promoting healthy digestion, oral health support, stimulating tissue regeneration, support for nerve healing, and oxygenation of your cells. With the many healing qualities available through essential oils, having them on hand can be quite essential (wink).

Let's talk chemistry for a moment. Essential oils are aromatic volatile liquids that are distilled from the most valuable part of the plant—they are far more powerful in this highly concentrated state than their dried herb cousins. Distilling shrubs, flowers, bushes, seeds, trees, and roots provides a unique chemical compound. You often need large quantities of plants to produce a single drop. In the case of rose oil, more than ten thousand pounds of rose petals are required to distill a single pound of essential oil. This is why a high-quality bottle of rose oil can be quite pricey.

There are multiple factors that determine the purity and quality of an essential oil, including the use of fertilizer and the soil conditions where the plants are grown, harvest location and methods, and the distillation process. Plant material that is used in creating a therapeutic oil should be free of herbicides and agrichemicals which otherwise could possibly react with the essential oil during the distillation process and produce toxic compounds. Be aware that many cheaper essential oils either have contaminants, such as heavy metals, synthetic chemicals, or other additives, or are a secondary distillation of the product.

Keep in mind that essential oils are vastly different than vegetable oils such as corn, olive, or peanut oil, and are not greasy or pore-clogging like their vegetable oil counter parts. Although vegetable oils can become rancid over time, high-quality, pure essential oils do not go rancid. In fact, if stored properly, away from sunlight and direct heat and cold, therapeutic-grade essential oils can last for many years.

You may have seen essential oils listed as an ingredient in personal care or household cleaning products. Although these aromatic contributors make for a refreshing scent, they often offer very little in the way of health benefits because they are typically purchased from lower-grade producers or from a second distillation process. These essential oils are often not therapeutic grade and should not be used topically or internally, as they are usually synthetic and therefore could be harmful. You are far better off finding quality personal care products and cleaning products that are organic and unscented and add a few drops of your favorite essential oils to the product yourself.

More and more scientific evidence and research shows the efficacy in the use of essential oils for healing practices. Essential oils penetrate the cell membranes and play an important role in assisting people to move beyond emotional barriers. The aldehydes and esters of many essential oils calm and soothe the central nervous system. This opens the door to relax and let go of emotions rather than building up anxiety and tension in the body. Remember, when you are in a stress response, the sympathetic nervous system is on high alert and the parasympathetic system, which supports healing and digestion, is not active. The aromatic molecules of essential oils absorb into the bloodstream from the nasal cavity to the limbic system. This, in turn, activates the amygdala and relaxes the sympathetic/parasympathetic system. Because essential oils affect the amygdala and pineal gland in the brain, they help the mind and body by releasing emotional trauma.

Each oil has a unique chemical structure offering a variety of benefits. The chemical structures aid in trauma release, wound care, immune system support, and emotional support. When using essential oils for your healing process it is crucial that you buy from a reputable, well-known source that offers certified therapeutic-grade oils.

There are three primary ways to integrate essential oils into your daily routine: internally, topically, and aromatically.

Internally: Certain oils have a history of culinary use and are supportive for dietary supplementation and overall wellness. Internal use of essential oils is the most potent way to use them, significantly more potent than ingesting the raw plant material they derive from. Therefore, proper dosing guidelines should be followed according to label recommendations. Most of the concern about internal use has to do with the effects of the oil on the mucosa, the membrane that lines various internal cavities. Some users believe that internal use is not safe. However, the internal use of thousands of users and modern research indicate the safety and efficacy of internal use when using a high-quality oil and following appropriate dosage guidelines.

Topically: The chemical structure of essential oils enables them to pass through the skin and the blood-brain barrier and be readily absorbed into the bloodstream, providing systemic support for your overall health. This systemic support is a key reason why the quality of oils is important. Topical uses include adding to massage treatments and personal care products, such as face cream and shampoo, or using directly as a part of massage or wound care, or as a skin treatment. Many oils can be safely applied neat (applied to the skin without a carrier oil); however, there are some oils that can cause a temporary hot/cold "burning" sensation or redness and should be applied with fractionated coconut oil, or other carrier oil to reduce sensitivity. It is always recommended to start slowly, beginning with one to two drops of your desired essential oil and build up as needed from there. Essential oils are very powerful, though, and only require a few drops for efficacy.

You can apply the oil directly over the area of concern, such as over the abdomen to reduce nausea, or on the bottom of the feet. When applying topically, avoid sensitive areas such as the eyes, nose, inner ears, genitals, and broken skin. If there is accidental contact in these areas, always apply a quality carrier oil to dilute the essential oil. Do not use water, as it can increase the intensity. If you get it in your eyes, apply a few drops of olive oil to a cotton ball and with your eyes gently closed, swipe the cotton ball over the area. Certain oils should not be used on babies or during pregnancy, although there are great benefits with some oils during this time. Consult your health care practitioner if you are pregnant or nursing before use.

Aromatically: Essential oils can be stimulating or calming depending on which oils are used. The aroma of any oil prompts powerful emotional, psychological, and biochemical responses by activating your olfactory system. The olfactory center is the only neural structure in the forebrain that takes input directly to the amygdala. There is also a direct connection between your nose and your brain's emotional control center known as the limbic system. Aromatic use of essential oils directly affects the limbic system, which controls mood, memory, and emotions. You've probably noticed this connection between smell and memories when you experience a scent that transports you through time, awakening memories as far back as early childhood. Our sense of smell is truly the strongest sense in the body.

Aromatic use of essential oils can be a powerful support for overall well-being and the immune system. The easiest way to use an oil aromatically is to simply remove the lid and inhale directly from the bottle. Or, apply a few drops to the palms of your hands and rub them together. Then cup your hands near your nose and mouth and inhale. To create a great aroma that benefits the whole room, add a few drops of oil to a diffuser. By adding a few drops of your chosen essential oils to a diffuser, the particles released purify the air, killing airborne pathogens, and improve the aroma of the room. Often a room takes on the odor of illness when someone is sick for an extended period. By adding a few drops of essential oils to a spray bottle of water, or by using a diffuser, the air is cleaner and lighter and smells delightful in a matter of a few moments.

Listed below are my top choices of essential oils to have on hand, along with their qualities and uses. I have selected them for their overall physical and emotional healing support, although there are many other oils that offer a variety of therapeutic support. I suggest you find a reputable source and start building your personal essential oil collection.

- **Bergamot:** Calming, neuro-tonic, anti-inflammatory, antidepressant, antibacterial, antifungal, digestive. May be used for endocrine health, depression, insomnia, nausea, vomiting, E. coli, muscle spasms, inflammation, stress, anxiety, respiratory infection, and urinary health. *

- **Clove:** Antioxidant, antibacterial, anti-inflammatory, antiviral, antifungal anti-parasitic, expectorant. May be used for toothache, pain relief, circulation, digestive health, high blood pressure, gout, parasites, arthritis, influenza, bacterial colitis, acne, and adrenal fatigue. *

- **Frankincense:** Anti-inflammatory, antidepressant,

immunostimulant, restorative. May be used for headaches, bronchitis, pneumonia, asthma, allergies, tonsillitis, relaxation, immune support, calming of the nervous system, jaundice, insomnia, Epstein-Barr virus, wound care, and tissue repair. *

- **Geranium:** Anti-inflammatory, regenerative, antitumoral, antiallergenic, detoxifier. May be used for skincare, bruising, hemorrhoids, liver detox, joint support, gallstones, nerve tonic, cardiovascular support, pancreatitis, liver disease, adrenal support, and hepatitis. *

- **Helichrysum:** Anti-inflammatory, regenerative, expectorant, detoxifier, neuroprotective, antispasmodic, anesthetic. May be used for dissolving blood clots, tissue repair, nerve tonic, scars, regenerative needs, liver problems, pancreatic support, and Parkinson's disease. *

- **Lavender:** Antibacterial, antidepressant, anti-inflammatory, soothing, relaxing, regenerative. May be used for convulsions, phlebitis, nausea, nerve calming, skin irritations, sleep support, anxiety, tension, burns, wound and tissue repair, allergies, and headache. *

- **Lemon:** Antioxidant, antiseptic, antibacterial, antifungal, mood enhancer. May be used for respiratory support, allergies, kidney stones, gallstones, strep throat, memory, depression, immune support, dehydration, renal failure, respiratory support, fevers, indigestion, and lymphedema. *

- **Lemongrass:** Anti-inflammatory, antimicrobial, anticarcinoma. May be used for vomiting, diarrhea, influenza, nerve pain, parasites, infections, cysts, kidney disorders, bladder infections, edema, fluid retention, tissue regeneration, and stomach spasms. *

- **Melaleuca (tea tree):** Antibacterial, antifungal, antiviral, anti-inflammatory, analgesic, neuro-tonic. May be used for parasites, ear aches, acne, bronchitis, influenza, allergies, and protecting against radiation. *

- **Myrrh:** Anti-inflammatory, antiviral, antimicrobial, antifungal.

May be used for tissue repair, skin conditions, bronchitis, diarrhea, viral hepatitis, wound care, sore throat, fibromyalgia, hemorrhoids, scars, stretch marks, wrinkles, influenza, emotional support, and oral care. *

- **Oregano:** Antiviral, antibacterial, antifungal, anti-infective. May be used for staph, strep throat, respiratory infections, allergies, inflammation, influenza, fibromyalgia, lupus, pneumonia, asthma, mold, parasites, herpes, hepatitis, melanoma, diverticulitis, and Epstein-Barr virus. *

- **Peppermint:** Anti-inflammatory, antispasmodic, invigorating, cooling, digestive. May be used for fever, depression, nerve regeneration, arthritis, joint and muscle discomfort, respiratory support, headache, colds, influenza, gout, fatigue, arthritis, and sinusitis. *

- **Rosemary:** Antibacterial, anti-infective, stimulant. May be used for arthritis, adrenal and chronic fatigue, dandruff, colds, influenza, viral infections, digestive issues, muscle aches and pains, neuropathy, muscle and bone pain, bronchitis, staff, strep throat, pancreatitis, pneumonia, yeast infections, and constipation. *

- **Wild orange:** Antioxidant, energizing, antidepressant, antiseptic. May be used for chronic fatigue syndrome, congestion, insomnia, tumor growth, grief, fibroid cysts, muscle aches, bronchitis, arthritis, bruises, fear, anxiety, and depression.*

- **Wintergreen:** Anti-inflammatory, analgesic. May be used for arthritis, backaches, gout, tendonitis, bladder infections, carpal tunnel, neuropathy, bronchitis, asthma, and chronic fatigue syndrome. *

*These statements have not been evaluated by the food and drug administration.

CHAPTER 9

Techniques for Personal Transformation

It is clear to any parent that children aren't born with an instruction manual. Even if they were, we would still spend much of our time winging it, quickly made aware that there are no cookie cutter rules to go by. Life is a learning curve no matter what we delve in to. Whether you are learning to play the piano or building a house, you will experience struggle in the transformation. It takes commitment and a desire to push beyond your comfort zone into uncharted territory. By placing your attention on your intentions, you create muscle memory to move you through the struggle from the unfamiliar into a new comfort zone that becomes familiar.

Life truly is simple. Not easy, but simple. It's our emotional attachment that we connect to experiences that makes life feel burdensome and challenging. When embracing a new level of development, it's common to feel overwhelmed with the daily input of internal and external pressure. The techniques in this chapter all have a core purpose in helping you with that pressure, by assisting you as you let go of the emotional weight of unresolved issues in your life and by bringing you greater clarity in moving forward.

I know the knee jerk response you may feel when someone suggests that you try a new technique to support your transformation. It goes something like this: "Yeah, that sounds good and all, but… you don't know how hard it's been and what I've gone through in my life."

Believe me when I say I've been there. There were about six years in my life prior to getting sick that I truly felt one of my greatest contributions to other people's lives was that they could look at me and think, "Thank God I don't have her life." I believed that I could give people hope to keep living with their challenges because mine felt so immense. The truth is, there were many people who told me that when they saw what my husband and I went through that they were indeed grateful for their own life.

Our lives were a living hell when my husband was wrongly accused for a crime he did not commit, set up for medical billing fraud because he was healing his patients and was a "threat" to the hospital. He was arrested and served five months in jail while he was trying to prove his innocence. I was pregnant with my fifth child at the time and we felt that no one understood how frightening it was. To this day I still struggle driving past a courthouse and refuse to watch any movie that involves a courtroom. Our finances were drained completely and the people who were supposedly helping us, stole all the legal documents from our file cabinet in an attempt to illegally transfer the titles for our home and vehicles to themselves. While my husband was in jail, I was within three days of losing our home, and our business was abandoned. Until then, I had never even met someone that served time in jail. I was desperate, isolated, and scared.

We lived in a picturesque neighborhood where every home was beautiful and every yard, manicured. We had always been friendly with our neighbors but not to the level of sharing details of personal experiences; not a single person in our neighborhood knew anything of the challenges we were facing. I didn't know who to trust and had no sense of security and belonging. Even after my husband returned home I was afraid that people would judge him so we lived quietly in our own private hell. I spent the next eight years so petrified that someone was coming to get him that I had debilitating panic attacks every time my doorbell rang. Not knowing who to trust, I was literally afraid of the world.

I know those years contributed an enormous amount to my emotional trauma. When I reflect on that time, I remember having a constant feeling of "gut rot." It literally felt like a boulder smashed against my gut and I was putrefying in a pool of my own fear. I know for a fact that those heavy emotions were truly the beginning of the breakdown of my health centered in my gut. I also know that I never want to feel that heaviness again, and because the trauma was so intense, I was willing to surrender to the possibility of transformation.

My first step was to clarify to myself that transformation does not need to be more suffering and pain, and it does not need to take months or years to unravel the chains of limitation. I invite you to do the same.

So, this is my one plug of tough love. Stop any thinking that resists transformation. Know that everyone has had challenges. Everyone is emotionally engaged with their own story and everyone has the potential to move into a healing space where they are no longer emotionally triggered by the past.

Events such as going through a divorce, losing a job, suffering a miscarriage, or having a car accident can pull the rug of emotional stability out from beneath you. They often elicit the question, "Why me?" Your past experiences may have caused you to feel that life isn't fair. And that sense was spot on—it's true, because life wasn't designed to be fair. Life is designed with challenges as an opportunity for growth and expansion. It is not our job to balance the scale between us and any other person. This would be an impossible feat anyway, because we do not know the reasons another soul chooses to go through what they do any more than you would know all the reasons that your soul chose to go through an illness. When I was aware of how often I was in the judgement seat with my limited perspective of other people's lives I knew that I had a shift to make. I recognized that I was unhappy in my own body and helpless in fixing myself, so I subconsciously put my attention outside of me.

It is easy to get trapped in a cycle of comparison and judgment which then can spiral into emotions of anger, pain, jealousy, and insecurity. In order for you to heal you will need to put your attention on your own experiences—and keep moving forward. Stop going back and replaying over and over why illness happened to you. This keeps you captive to the past and focused on the problem, stuck in the vibration of illness, jealousy, isolation, pain, and fear. Instead, shift toward healing your past and taking responsibility for your own experience. Find the opportunities in this moment, remembering that in all aspects of life, internal growth happens when you experience discord and the feeling of having stability pulled out from beneath you. A great way to move your experience toward healing and growth is with the tools for personal transformation included in the following pages.

You may still feel some resistance to the techniques I'm offering. Despite the fact that everything I have shared with you has provided great benefit to others, you may have put a subconscious limit on what you think can help you.

Here is a common conversation exchange between a person searching for answers (A) and someone who is offering tools for support (B):

(A) Hey, I am desperate and willing to do anything to heal. I heard you may be able to help me. What do you offer?

(B) Great, I would be honored to support you. I have proven techniques that I have seen assist hundreds of people. It's really quite simple and just takes commitment and dedication to change your life.

This statement seems benign enough, but just woke the sleeping tiger. Fears rise to the surface, as person (A)'s amygdala begins sounding the alarm. In order to protect themselves, (A) shares an exhaustive list of what they have experienced and why they can't be helped. Subconsciously they are saying, "It might have worked for someone else but it's not possible for me." I invite you to try to open yourself up beyond this resistance. To trust and give it a go anyway…

As great as it would be to simply read these techniques and suddenly be healed, it does takes more effort than that. I assure you, though, it's worth your time to delve deeper in uncovering and healing the past. You may find that when your awareness of one incident is expanded that other seemingly unrelated issues become more clear. I am not claiming that all of these techniques will work for every person, but be willing to try them. Don't feel that for you to have a deeper understanding of your past you will need to spend hours wailing and thrashing as you release your history of trauma. Most of these techniques take little more than five to ten minutes to get some valuable insight. However, years of trauma does take time to release. Above all else, be patient and kind with yourself.

Each of these techniques are ones that I use myself and have used with my mentoring clients. I encourage you to have a pen and notebook or journal nearby to document your aha moments, insight, and wisdom. You will notice that I suggest closing your eyes during any visual technique. This is important so that you can eliminate external visual distractions and focus your attention within.

As you move through the techniques, trust your intuition—this is going to be your most valuable tool.

A PLEA FOR LOVE

This technique is helpful in releasing emotional pain associated with guilt, unworthiness, or shame, which can be debilitating and prevent healing from taking place.

We've all had times where we replayed an experience that we just can't seem to let go of over and over through our heads. After a while these thoughts take on a life of their own, becoming bigger than the actual experience itself. When a person continually goes over the story of an unresolved experience, it is often because of a hidden belief in self-punishment. When this is the case, it may be valuable to move your attention outside of your body and have something to anchor to as a way of connecting to love.

Think of the most nurturing individual you can that exudes love, compassion, and kindness. Who would that be for you? Some suggestions are Jesus, Mother Mary, Mother Theresa, God, or the Dalai Lama. You may recognize that some of their most beautiful qualities are forgiveness and acceptance. Once you have someone in mind, find something near you in nature that you are drawn to as a symbolic representation of this individual. This can be a tree, a large boulder, or a backyard pond—whatever you choose will be used as your spiritual proxy to this person that personifies love.

Stand in front of your proxy and share why you feel guilt, shame, or that you are unworthy of love. Say out loud everything that you are feeling. How you screwed up and why you don't deserve compassion and why you believe you are not worthy of forgiveness. This is your raw and real moment where you get to plead your case of being unlovable and unworthy. Go into detail about mistakes that you made and share your guilt, shame, and self-deprecation. Keep saying it until it is all out of you. Once you have purged all the negative emotions, take a deep breath and close your eyes, then ask for forgiveness. Although it is not the tree or Mother Theresa that is forgiving you, they will hold that intention as you begin to forgive yourself.

Listen to the reply of love, compassion, and forgiveness. If your thoughts go toward self-condemnation on any level you must go back to releasing. I guarantee whatever deed is holding you back could never warrant imprisoning yourself away from healing. To believe otherwise is an unhealthy mindset trying to convince you of what is not true. Take a few deep breaths and listen to the reply from your chosen nurturing individual. Recognize that their ability to forgive comes from their deep level of compassion. Commit to make right anything that you have done to cause harm to yourself or any other individual.

We all have experienced shame and guilt. Commit to letting the past go and receive the compassion that will allow your healing to take place. Understand that you are a gift from God, here to experience life fully. Feel the love washing over you and releasing any emotions that are causing you pain. Visualize the words "shame," "guilt," and "unworthiness" leaving your body and transmuting into light. Take a few moments to write down the loving response you received and refer to it often until it becomes your new truth.

WRITE A LETTER TO YOUR BODY

I love the powerful breakthroughs that can happen with this technique—it is an amazing way to open up communication with your body.

All health concerns are a physical manifestation of an area that is out of balance. By setting the intention of communicating with your body on paper you can open up a dialogue and get a greater understanding of the messages your body has been trying to tell you all along.

This is a very simple technique that only requires a notebook, pen, and some quiet time alone. You can either write your letter to your body as a whole or to a specific body part that is out of balance. You can even write a letter to a part that is no longer present. I know people who have written letters to a breast lost due to a mastectomy or a letter to the uterus that is no longer there because of a hysterectomy. Although that part of the body is no longer physically present, its energy is very much still present and trying to communicate to you. This is the case when a finger or a limb is lost in an accident and phantom pain occurs. Begin your letter by writing, "Dear _____," (fill in the blank with an area of your body that you want to communicate with). Then share your emotions, ask questions, and open up the dialog with your body in any way you need.

Once you have finished writing your letter, turn over the page and respond from the viewpoint of your body. Tapping into your intuition, listen for any thoughts or emotions that your body has about you. Your body may share that it feels ignored, that you haven't taken proper care of it to recover. It may share fear or anger as well. Listen to any suggestions that your body is making to assist in the healing process. Feel free to continue the conversation as you see fit.

PEEL THE ONION

You may have moments, days, weeks, or even months when you just simply don't feel like yourself. It often takes little more than experiencing recurrent symptoms to cause a downward spiral into fear, anger, or frustration with your body and your life. When you notice these emotions come up, remind yourself that emotions are the body's messenger. Tune in to what your body is trying to say to you.

Emotions have layers. Recognize an emotion that you are feeling and peel the onion back to the root. Pay particular attention to any patterns that may show up. Was there an event or person that caused the emotion? It may seem like a benign incident but choose to look at it. Was it a call from your mother, a coworker's new relationship, your sister posting on Facebook about her next great adventure?

For me, my emotional issues were in relation to other people eating food that I couldn't. When I ate at home, I had more control over my environment and was content with the limited food I ate. Because of severe allergies that I had developed and the need to heal the lining of my gut, I was on a strict dietary protocol. I was dairy-free, soy-free, gluten-free, and grain-free. I ate organic and zero processed food. This was usually okay because there were still plenty of foods I liked available to me—it didn't hurt my stomach to eat an avocado or to drink a smoothie. But put me in a restaurant where everyone was ordering delicious-looking foods that I couldn't touch, haphazardly sharing food and eating without a second thought, and ending their meal and never once wondering if it was going to hurt them caused me to feel like a victim—a self-loathing, depressed, and jealous woman. It made me feel sad that I was left out and nervous that others were judging me. I wanted to explain myself by saying, "I'm not eating that because I will start vomiting and have severe diarrhea and stomach cramping for three days," but knew that with that level of sharing it wouldn't take long for me to be removed from the invite list as a downer. I suck at pretending I am "fine" when I am not. Obviously, being a hermit and missing out on the joys that other people were living to avoid these situations only deepened my depression and isolation. So, I had to address these emotions head on and peel my own onion. I recognized that I was being triggered because of emotions that were rooted in the past that were now surfacing as emotional pain.

Now consider what emotions in your own life you would like to take a deeper look at. What do you feel may be behind them?

If you have trouble identifying the root of these emotions, try putting pen to paper to work through the layers of your onion.

1st layer: This is the surface layer that is obvious. Are you jealous, sad, or angry? Start there and then you'll need to go a little deeper. Start by writing, "I feel _____ *(fill in the blank with your emotion that you feel)* when _____ *(fill in with the person or event that is related to the emotion).*" As an example, "I feel jealous when other people eat foods that I cannot." Continue to write out the emotions that you are feeling until it feels complete. Stay with it. Be specific and don't worry about editing. This is for your eyes only.

2nd layer: Start a new paragraph or turn the page. Think about other times that you felt triggered with a similar emotion. What people were involved and why did they trigger you? You may not think of something right away but drop into the feeling and have patience. Write it out. Add any other emotions that come up and express them on the paper, continuing to write until you feel that you got it all out.

3rd layer: Most often a specific incident, person, or group of people are involved with the original source of that emotion. The next step is to write a letter to the incident or the person/people involved, even if they are no longer living or if you have not had contact for many years, to create closure and allow healing to take place. (You will not send this letter.) Include in your letter that you are ready to let go of the emotional attachments to the experience. Feel free to express whatever comes up for you. When you have finished, turn the page and write a letter to yourself from the viewpoint of the other person or situation, responding to your original letter and asking for forgiveness. Explore what may have prompted past behavior or conditions that hurt you. Many times, the root of an emotional trigger is often from a childhood experience. Remember that children can be cruel and have a limited perspective. Have compassion for yourself and gratitude for your new understanding and willingness to let go.

FREE PASS DAY

Sometimes in life we need an opportunity to get off the emotional roller coaster, and give ourselves the opportunity to recalibrate and decide our next step. When your emotions have built up so much that it feels as if you're swimming upstream, then it is time to schedule yourself a free pass day. This is a day when you give yourself twenty-four hours to say, "All bets are off." Remove everyone else from your schedule. No doctor appointments, no counseling sessions, no health concerns. In your world, for the next twenty-four hours, live as if there are no problems, no illness, no disease, and no obligations. Decide for yourself what the healthiest person you know would do on their day off. And go do it.

Having a free pass is more than just giving yourself permission to throw caution to the wind. It's about stepping off the train of frustration and away from your problems to gain a greater perspective and realign with your desires. When you have more clarity and are free of limitations, you can make decisions about your health from a higher-minded space—seeing that it is possible to be healthy. By having a day when you *act* healthy, you can condition the cells of your body to believe that this is true, opening you to a new vibrational frequency. Raising your perspective opens the door for more insight and wisdom that you didn't see before.

The only rule to a free pass is YOU CANNOT DO ANYTHING THAT WILL PUT YOUR HEALTH OR BODY IN JEOPARDY. For me, this means that I don't go and eat a large bowl of pasta and garlic bread to prove to my body that it can safely eat gluten, but I can go out to lunch with friends at a restaurant that serves gluten-free options, reminding myself that very healthy people opt for gluten-free eating all the time. If you are on any medication or regimen with your health practitioner, then run your plans past them to make sure you aren't going to do anything that will be detrimental to your health. The common-sense position with this is to keep taking any medications that you need for your health and avoid eating or drinking things that you know hurt your body. But for all other aspects, throw your hands up in the air, roll the windows down, crank the music up, and live a full day completely healthy, vibrant, and whole.

YOUR INNER CHILD

This is a visualization technique that helps you connect to the innocence that once resided within you and access deeper emotions that may have been hidden in recent years. This technique can also assist in generating more self-love and compassion as you struggle with healing.

Sit comfortably and close your eyes. Take a few breaths to relax your mind. Visualize yourself going back in time and standing in front of your childhood home. If you moved many times when you were a child choose the home that you lived in between the ages of seven to ten years old. Notice the yard and whether there are any trees, shrubs, or grass. Is there a sidewalk that leads up to the front door? Is the yard well-manicured or overgrown? Are there toys strewn across the yard? Is your home a single dwelling, in an apartment complex, or a trailer in a trailer park? Are you in the city, with multiple homes on small lots and a lot of traffic, or are you in the country, with plenty of room to roam? Visualize that it's a beautiful sunny day and no one else is around. Spend some time visually scanning the area around your home and notice any emotions that come up. Is there a longing to run in and reconnect with what was, or are you more inclined to move on knowing that it was in the past? Who else lived in the home with you? If, in the present, your parents have passed on, your heart may have a longing to go back in time. To smell your mother's perfume again or to hear your father's voice as he comes home from a day of work. Walk up to the front door and place your hand on the door knob. Feel the solidness of the knob in your grip. Open the door and enter the home, noting if anything stands out to you. Are you in the entryway or in the middle of an open floor plan? Do you notice any sounds or scents from the past? Make note of the furniture or if there are photos hanging on the wall. Recall each family member that lived here with you. What was the relationship that you had with the other members of your family? Did you receive love from them or did the relationship feel more strained or distant?

Now, visualize yourself entering your childhood bedroom. As you enter the room, imagine seeing your child self in the room. What is your child self doing? What does he or she look like? Notice his or her hair and clothes. Is your child self well-groomed and clean or in need of a good bath? How do you feel about this child? Do you feel inclined to nurture your child self or push him or her away? Pay special attention to any judgment or criticism you feel toward your child self.

What emotions does your child self feel? Does he or she love life and have a lot of friends or feel alone? What message would you like to share to give this child a sense of hope? Tell your child self that you would like to talk to them. Share your message with your child self and then ask him or her to share a message with you as well. Trust your intuition and listen to the message from your child self. Once you have received your message give your child self an affectionate embrace. Tell him or her that you love them and that you will not abandon them.

As you come out of this visualization, internally ask if you're living the life that you promised yourself when you were young. Did you have hopes and dreams to do more with your life than what you are doing now? Did your life turn out better or worse than you expected? Are there adjustments that you should make to be more in alignment with your authentic self? Take some time to journal about this along with any messages that your child self shared with you.

MEETING YOUR FUTURE SELF

You've probably seen interviews where a celebrity is asked, "What advice would you give your younger self now that you've made it?" This is often followed up with answers such as, "It's going to be okay." Or, "Hang in there. It gets better." Or, "Take that leap of faith. It will be worth it." We can't exactly go back in time to share our more mature wisdom with our younger selves; however, time is not linear and all the wisdom that we desire is truly accessible when we choose to tap into it.

This technique is a very simple imagery experience where you imagine meeting with your future self to support you in gaining clarity in your life. I encourage you to have specific questions that you want to address with your future self. Again, I would like to remind you to trust your intuition. While it's no guarantee that the information you receive is exactly how your life is going to play out, there is always wisdom available from this experience. You may recognize that an outcome mentioned by your future self is a possibility under the circumstances that you are currently in.

If you see a possible outcome that you don't like or one that causes some anxiety, remember that you have free agency and can take steps to change the outcome. This experience, in fact, can be an ideal opportunity to ask your future self what changes you should make for a better outcome, or ask for guidance with a specific situation, such as, "Which treatment is best for me at this time?'

Having a notebook or journal nearby, write down a few questions that you would like insight on. Having the questions written down will help you have more focus and clarity regarding the direction that you want to go.

Sit in a comfortable position. Close your eyes and focus on your breathing. Place your attention on your toes. With each inhale and exhale continue to move up your body, relaxing any tension or tightness that you may be feeling. Release the tension in your calves, your thighs, your hips, and your abdomen. Let go of any stress and tension and allow your belly to fully relax. Move up to your chest. Breath in slow, rhythmic breaths. Inhale and exhale, releasing the tension in your shoulders and allow all that tension to wash down your arms, through your hands, and out through the tips of your fingers. Bringing your attention to your face, relax all the tiny muscles there. Move your attention to the top of your head. Visualize a tube of light connecting you to God's energy and feel a protective and healing energy wash over you. On your next inhalation, visualize a gentle release from your physical body that moves you into the tube of light. As you enter the tube of light, hold your attention on the date that you want to meet your future self. It can be three months, one year, five years, or twenty years from now. I recommend that you practice with different time frames, although it is not necessary to choose a specific time. If you would like, you can allow the visual process to take you to the most appropriate time and place for your greatest insight. It may be helpful to just project to the near future if you are in a very weakened state. If you are undergoing a medical treatment where you are anticipating a long healing journey, then extend the time frame of this experience further out. Notice that the tube of light is moving forward and carrying you with it. Imagine that the environment beneath you is shifting. You may travel to another home or outside in nature. Trust that the tube of light will take you to the place for your highest good. Allow the tube to stop at the appropriate time and place.

Now, visualize yourself coming back to the ground. As you do, notice the new environment. What specific items stand out to you? Is there different furniture? Are you in a home that you've never been to before or is this place familiar? Get very comfortable in this environment and notice your future self approaching you. If this future self is in the near future, you may look similar to how you look now. If this is five years or longer in the future, notice the clothes that your future self is wearing, or a change in hairstyle. Have a conversation with your future self. Is he or she healthy and vibrant and strong? Ask your questions and listen for the intuitive answers. Remember that your future-self wants what's best for you. Open up the dialog for any unresolved concerns you may be having until you feel complete. When you have finished, thank your future self for the guidance and return your attention back to current time. As you open your eyes, take a few moments to write down any insights and suggestions. Follow up by taking the appropriate steps to move forward.

FLIP THE SWITCH

This technique is very simple and only takes a moment, but can be extremely powerful in redirecting your focus of attention. Every one of us has shortcomings and we tend to beat ourselves up when we do something that we regret. This, in turn, causes self-judgment and criticism. By calling it out for what it is, humanness, you can forgive yourself faster and have greater compassion for yourself. In this humanness, you will find that there is an underlying goodness in you that happens to be overshadowed at the moment. By flipping the switch you are turning off the negative thoughts and illuminating the positive within you.

If I am doing this technique while I am alone then I personally like to vocalize out loud the following steps, but if others are around it's just as effective having a quick internal dialogue. The important component in doing this exercise is to catch yourself in self-judgement and criticism, while the emotions are still present. One of my greatest spiritual teachers, Katherine Beck, taught me that it takes ninety seconds for an emotion to settle into your body. If you have awareness of a negative emotion in your body and are able to catch it within ninety seconds, redirect the energy rather than reacting to it and you will have the greatest benefit. I suggest that you work through this exercise on paper the first few times that you do it to help pull unconscious thoughts up and give you more clarity.

When you notice a negative emotion, or thought, begin by saying, "I forgive myself for_____." (You are recognizing an adjustment that needs to be made within and calling it out rather than allowing it to have power over you.)

Then say, "I love myself for_____." (This gives you an opportunity to have self-compassion and focus on your great qualities.)

Lastly, say, "Now I choose_____." (This statement reminds you that no one is perfect but we have free agency to make better choices.)

As an example, one of the issues where I often feel regret is when I'm busy taking care of multiple tasks and feel distracted when my children need my attention.

In this instance, I might say, "I forgive myself for being distracted when my children need me." Then, "I love myself for accomplishing tasks that need to get done in a timely manner." And lastly, "Now I choose to improve upon my time management so that I am fully present for my family."

This also gives me an opportunity for self-improvement by prompting me to make adjustments as I recognize a need for them, without the harshness of self-judgement or criticizing myself for being a "bad" parent.

CHAPTER 10

Protecting Your Health from Toxins

As discussed so far in this book, healing begins from within and is greatly affected by your beliefs, thoughts and emotions, and diet. But, there is another key component that needs to be addressed—toxic exposure. Toxins enter our bodies through the food we eat, the air we breathe, the products we use, and the water we drink. Toxin exposure can potentially increase the possibility of a long-term compromised immune system, and has been repeatedly linked to a variety of chronic ailments, including Parkinson's disease and cancer.

To support your healing process, I feel that it is important to guard yourself from any additional stress on your body by limiting your exposure to toxic chemicals. I have listed below potential sources of toxin exposure and encourage you to adjust your lifestyle as you see necessary.

Potential Toxins in Your Home

Ideally, a person's home is a safe haven from the outside world. A place where we gather with loved ones, replenish our bodies and spirits with rest and nourishing food. In our modern era we have filled our homes with chemical-laden products for nearly every room in the house. While everyone has the right to choose which products they use, I think it is valuable to be educated on potential side effects of chemical exposure in your environment. I have listed below possible sources to take into consideration.

Fabric softener and dryer sheets: Few among us can dispute the joy of pulling a fresh load of laundry out of the dryer and holding the warm fabric up to smell that "fresh laundry" scent. For me, this was one of the simple pleasures of taking care of a household—inhaling freshness for a moment. Although it may be delightful to smell fresh laundry, fabric softener is not a healthy way to do it. Fabric softener is considered the number one cause of indoor pollution. The scent that you are inhaling is often a toxic dose of VOC (volatile organic compounds). A healthier alternative is purchasing wool laundry balls to use in your dryer, which will help keep your laundry soft. If you love that fresh laundry smell, place a few drops of your favorite essential oil on the wool balls as you start a new load in the dryer. This will not only make your laundry smell amazing, but the laundry room too.

Antibacterial soap: Almost all antibacterial soaps contain the chemical triclosan. Triclosan has long been used in commercial cleaning products for hospitals and care centers. However, it was introduced in home cleaning products during the 1990s. Triclosan is known to inhibit the growth of various bacteria, but its claimed superiority to regular soap in preventing illness or reducing bacteria on your hands has been disputed. It isn't worth the risk! Triclosan and other chemical agents are known to disrupt thyroid function and hormone levels, and furthermore, health experts believe that overuse of antibacterial chemicals promote the growth of bacteria that become resistant to antibacterial treatment.

Synthetic fragrance: Nearly every chemical in synthetic fragrance is derived from petrochemicals. These chemical toxins are known to disrupt hormone activity and cause cancer, birth defects, nervous system disorders, and allergies. Petrochemicals have also been linked to diabetes and obesity. Manufacturers in the United States can legally hide hundreds of synthetic chemicals under the guise of "fragrance" without revealing what those ingredients are. These fragrances are most common in laundry detergent, fabric softener, dryer sheets, cleaning supplies, personal care products, and scented candles.

Household cleaning products: Product manufacturers are not required by federal law to list ingredients on their labels. Ammonia is known to trigger asthmatic attacks and oven cleaner is known to cause damage to children who come in contact with it. Every year people get third-degree burns of the throat and esophagus from exposure to these and other toxic cleaners. People often believe that to be "clean" it takes harsh chemicals, but this isn't the case. Many products available today have the same benefits as conventional cleaners but without the toxic cost on your body. You can find product safety ratings by searching the Environmental Working Group (EWG) database at ewg.org. EWG has researched more than two thousand common cleaning products and ranks these products on a scale indicating the level of concern posed by exposure to their ingredients. Look for products with an A rating for a safer alternative to toxic chemicals.

Flame retardants: The United States implemented fire safety standards in the 1970s which adopted the use of toxic, flame-retardant chemicals. These chemicals are now widely used in furniture foam, electronics, draperies, and upholstery. Many infant products, such as nursing pillows, high chairs, cribs, strollers, car seats and bassinets, are also coated in flame retardants. These chemicals are added to everyday household products to slow the ignition rate of flame growth in the event of a fire, giving you more time to escape. Although, in theory, flame retardants could be life-saving, they certainly don't stop a fire that is in progress.

Understandably, every second counts, but as helpful as flame retardants could possibly be during a fire, their negative health impact at other times makes them problematic. The chemical molecules of the flame retardants do not absorb and dissipate but rather are collected in dust and inhaled. Flame retardants are hormone disruptors and are associated with infertility, thyroid problems, and learning disabilities. You can limit this impact by keeping dust under control and use a high-quality air filter in your home. But if possible, it's preferable to find products without these added chemicals. Manufacturers are not required to disclose the chemicals they use to make their products as long as they comply with safety regulations, so you're not likely to find this information easily unless a manufacturer is touting a product's non-toxic qualities. To avoid these chemicals, seek out "green" building materials, carpeting, furniture, and upholstery that state they do not use fire retardants. Although you will pay more for organic materials, the payoff is often worth it.

Potential Toxins in Your Environment

Environmental toxins include naturally occurring compounds such as lead, mercury, radon, formaldehyde, and cadmium, as well as man-made chemicals such as BPA, phthalates, and pesticides. Many of these toxins are known to cause cancer, act as endocrine disruptors, contribute to developmental problems, and cause organ failure.

Environmental groups have uncovered dangerous levels of environmental toxins in water and food supplies, building materials, and agriculture use. People often mistakenly assume that if they don't work or live in the worst-affected areas that they are safe from toxic chemical exposure. However, even low levels of exposure over time can cause damage to your liver. In today's world our livers are already taking a tremendous hit with constant exposure to harmful cleaning and personal care products, medications, and processed foods. This causes an increased strain on your body's detoxification organs, which can potentially lead to fatty liver disease—a condition that affects one in every four Americans, according to some estimates.

People also tend to discount their use and consumption of pesticides. Pesticides are any substance used to kill or repel weeds or insects, and exposure to them over a lifetime can have detrimental effects in your healing process. It must be noted that most conventional food production uses high levels of pesticides which we then ingest in our diet. In the United States, over 4.5 billion pounds of pesticides and herbicides are used each year. This is astronomical.

To limit your exposure to pesticides, I suggest you buy organic food whenever possible or, better yet, grow your own. The fresh air, the connection to Mother Earth, and the act of cultivating life by growing fresh produce can give a real sense of purpose and gratification. If you buy produce, organic or conventional, you should wash all fruits and vegetables with a veggie wash to remove any pesticide residue. You can minimize your exposure to pesticides from commercially treated lawns and sidewalks by having family members and visitors leave their shoes at the door rather than tracking in harmful toxins that have been picked up outside.

Potential Toxins in Your Body

There are many supplements available at health food stores that are specifically formulated to remove toxins from the body. I recommend you find a reputable nutritionist or health practitioner that can assist you in detoxing and rebuilding your body, remembering that if you have a compromised immune system, you will need to detox slowly and gently.

Detoxing often includes removing heavy metals, parasites, fungi, bacteria, and viruses. Be aware that these are not a one-time fix type of treatment. Parasite cleanses often take many months due to the multiple stages of the parasite life-cycle, in which eggs can remain dormant for an extended time. These eggs often don't hatch until the adult parasite dies off. Parasites can be undetectable and microscopic, but don't be fooled to believe they won't have a negative impact on your health. Most people aren't aware they even have parasites in their system. It wasn't until I was very ill that we even considered this as an option for me, even though my husband is a brilliant speaker on the topic and our herb store sells a great deal of parasite cleanses every month. A parasite cleanse is a simple detoxification protocol that often involves black walnut, cloves, and wormwood, which are known to kill a great majority of common parasites. Practitioners will often supplement a cleanse with a plant-based enzyme to break down the encapsulation that our bodies usually produce to wall off the parasites from our system, and other herbal products to support the channels of elimination. A typical parasite cleanse may utilize a two-week protocol to kill off adult parasites. Then, your practitioner may suggest the use of antifungal, antibacterial, or antiviral herbal products for two weeks while waiting for the parasite eggs to hatch. Then, finish by repeating the parasite protocol once again.

Please consult a knowledgeable care provider if you suspect parasites may be in your system to recommend specific products for your care and for any suggested dosing.

Protecting Yourself

Your body's ability to process and eliminate toxin exposure is dependent on a healthy and well-functioning system. There are physicians who claim that we don't need to do anything about the toxins we are exposed to because we have a liver that takes care of anything we encounter. This is an ignorant and potentially dangerous point of view. As noted above, our livers are indeed incredibly valuable in processing toxic chemicals but years of overload can take quite a toll on liver function. According to Medical Medium Anthony William, nine out of ten people today have a sluggish liver. Symptoms related to a sluggish liver include acne, weight gain, eczema, psoriasis, bloating, brain fog, and emotional disturbance, specifically anger. In an optimal state your liver breaks down the chemical compounds into simpler compounds to be removed via one of your body's four channels of elimination: your skin, respiratory system, urinary system, and gastrointestinal system. In short, you can strengthen your body's function and minimize any added stress by removing exposure of potential hazards.

Increasing your water intake to help flush out toxins and using a high-quality air filter in your home can help a great deal. Make sure your water is free of contaminants by using a quality water filter and replacing air filters often. Limiting processed foods that are often full of chemicals, sugar, and trans-fat and increasing fresh organic produce is a step in the right direction. Additionally, there are several supplements available in herb stores for detoxification. Consult a naturopath or health practitioner that is educated in supplements and detoxification for a liver detox program. Traditionally, medical doctors are not trained or educated in nutrition and herbal supplement use—specifically, because of big pharma. Medications, by and large, are chemicals that are challenging for the liver to process. If you are on medications, consult your physician about the risks associated and see if there are alternatives that are safer for you to try.

CHAPTER 11

Experiencing and Measuring Success

Although this book is geared specifically toward healing and improving your physical body, you may have caught on to my hidden agenda in encouraging you to strive for improvements in multiple areas of your life. Why? Because if you strive for an improvement in *any* area of your life, the impact from the changes you make, such as having higher self-esteem or a clearer sense of purpose and direction, adjusts your vibrational frequency so you can begin to attract other higher vibrational frequencies into your life. Thus, providing you a clearer vision of what is possible, which will contribute to your success in *all* areas of your life—including your health.

We are designed to strive, grow, and enhance our personal development. When we stop searching for self-improvement, we may have symptoms of depression set in. When we go through phases where we feel stuck and lack purpose, an internal mechanism activates within us and we start looking outside of ourselves for something more. It's common to have depression knocking at your door when you're already battling illness. Do your best to keep it away by instigating forward movement in life. By setting goals that are measurable, your brain recognizes accomplishment and gives you a sense that you are experiencing success.

There are five specific areas for a well-rounded individual to improve upon and create success: health, relationships, financial stability, spiritual connection, and skill improvement. Choose one of these areas where you have potential for improvement and set a goal. You may think that a health goal is the obvious choice based upon the book that you are reading right now, but that isn't always the case. Sometimes, when you have been struggling with a health challenge for an extended period, it can be refreshing to shift your focus away from a health-centered journey to something new, with the understanding that improving any area of your life naturally puts you in "improvement mode." For some, negative internal dialogue comes into play and you think, "Meh, why bother?" Thankfully, you are reading this book, which means that you have hope. (Especially if you made it this far in the book. Kudos, by the way.) If you struggle coming up with a goal related to your health, then choose one of the other areas for success. Maybe, choose a goal related to relationships. Options within this area could be to improve relationships with extended family, strengthen your marriage, or spend quality time with your children and commit to telling them that you love them every day. Goals don't have to be large to be effective.

Begin by making a list of everything that you desire to improve in your life. If it's easier, list these goals in the separate categories noted above. Only choose one or two to work on initially. Anything more can feel overwhelming and scatter your attention, which can cause you to sabotage yourself from doing them at all. Have the intention to push yourself out of your comfort zone but also keep success within reach. One of my first goals was to be able to walk to my mailbox and back without stopping because of weakness and exhaustion. Other goals were to integrate a variety of foods back into my diet, to meditate regularly, and to spend quality time with each of my children. Eventually, my goals expanded to having the strength to play a game of basketball with my kids and to travel out of town without being sick. Now, here I am writing this book and accomplishing my biggest goal yet.

Be crystal clear in what you want to achieve. Two common goals that people initially set are to lose weight and have more money. But, what exactly does that mean? Do you want an extra $500 or $5,000 a week? Do you want to lose 12 pounds or 120 pounds? Remember, the field of creation is always working with you and if you aren't clear as to what you are asking for, the Universe isn't clear either.

Once you have clear vision of what you want then you need to write it down. Take some time to look at what you put down on the piece of paper. Does it seem doable or a fantasy? Again, notice your emotional state. Does it scare you or excite you? How much do you want that goal? Rate your desire to reach it from 1 to 10, with 1 being "I wrote down the first thing that popped in my head because my spouse/business partner/mother wants me to do this but I could care less" and 10 being a knockout, home run level of excitement where you can say, "I want this goal so much that I eat, breathe, and sleep with it swirling in my head. I feel it running through my blood and know 100 percent that it is on its way." If you are a 10 way to go! If not, then be real with yourself and remember that there is no wrong answer. Choosing a number gives you a base to launch from.

Now, what do you need to do to reach your goal? Do you need more education, a support team, a mentor or personal coach, more time or money? Write these down as well because you will need to know what it takes to accomplish what you want. Decide what steps you will take each day until you've succeeded. Stay accountable by enlisting someone to report to and take steps toward your goal, daily. It's not the size of the steps you take that matter but rather the implementation of consistency in creating a pattern for success. If your goal is to walk to the mailbox and back like mine was, maybe set a goal to do it a little faster or a little further each day.

The next step is to clarify in your mind a vision of that goal attained. This may be accomplished more easily by finding a picture that closely represents what you desire and spend time memorizing the image. Remember to place this on your vision board. If you haven't created one yet, get on it. Doing so will assist you in creating the internal image.

It's not always going to be easy, but to move forward in life takes dedication. So, the next important element is to decide on your "Why?" Being clear on why you want to accomplish your goal will activate very specific emotions to support you in success. Remember, emotions are the driving force of creation. In Viktor Frankl's book, *Man's Search for Meaning*, he shares one of my favorite quotes, "Those who have a *why* to live, can bear with almost any *how*." By getting clear with your why, you activate the how to appear.

Be gentle on yourself when setbacks happen. You may have glimpses of hope and then feel shattered when that hope is dashed. Growth and healing, though, are not a linear path. And neither is attaining a new goal. Often you will travel sideways and backward and even stall before you arrive. There is opportunity in all of this as well. Setbacks can strengthen your resolve and help you to clarify deeper what you desire. Growth, learning, and expansion are what we are here to experience. By setting goals and attaining goals you are on your way to experience all three.

It would be greatly beneficial for you to measure your progress. Setting small, attainable goals and tracking success not only gives you a sense of accomplishment, but trains your amygdala to look for success in your healing by moving attention away from your past experiences. Keep a journal or notebook to document this success. (Seriously, you should have a journal by now. If not, make that your first goal.) Every day write down what steps you will take toward your goal. Each new day document whether or not you did those steps, and stay out of excuses or a victim mentality. If you noticed that you're not working toward your goal, then it's time to ask yourself if this is where your attention should be or what is holding you back. Sometimes, when there is a stall in forward movement, it is either because of a fear of the unknown future, the perceived loss in accomplishing the goal, or a lack of clear vision of the accomplished goal.

Allow me to segue for a bit to why seeing success is more valuable than you might think. There are many opportunities to share with others what it feels like to be sick, and when we are ill we usually take those opportunities. We update the doctor, the pharmacist, our mailman, our friends, and the beautician on our latest pitfalls and before long, your moments of despair become bragging rights of endurance. Why are we so driven to share our story over and over? First of all, from an emotional sense, illness and pain are a connecting force, opening up empathy in others and providing us with a sense of value. Second, as noted earlier, your brain is designed to look for danger. It is one of the most rudimentary aspects of the human brain. For your brain to know what may or may not be a dangerous interaction that may or may not kill you, your brain will register traumatic or unpleasant experiences and retain these memories front and center, to access at any chance encounter with danger (perceived or real). So, these traumatic experiences are etched in deeply. Furthermore, with traumatic illness or chronic pain your mind can't make sense as to why you are still not healed and therefore keeps you in the seeking mode for answers. This is why Aunt Millie at the annual family reunion continues to repeat the same stories about her husband that died five years earlier. On some level, her brain is still trying to understand why he isn't with her anymore, even though she knows on the physical level that he died (which you know because you saw her standing at his casket during the funeral). Due to the trauma of loss, her mind has not fully put the pieces together. In other words, there is a disconnect in the neural pathways of her brain. She may have held in her subconscious mind that he would always be there to take care of her, or remembered the commitment to being together forever, but now that he is no longer with her, she has to keep talking about it until that part of her brain can feel resolution.

The brain stores and recalls memory based upon association. The more emotional the memory is, the quicker and easier those associations are made. That is why we see people having long-lasting anxiety when, on the outside there doesn't appear to be any real threat. Accessing a triggered memory isn't just recalling an old memory buried in your brain but more of an unconscious reflex, something that can happen without trying. The only way to heal this is to make new associations—by setting goals and seeing success.

Seeing documented success (however incremental) is also motivating. While each of us have our own definition of success in life and in healing, by taking action, committing to regaining your health, and charting your progress, rather than just deciding to "see how it goes," you become purposeful in your daily activities. For me, I lost a lot of muscle tone spending months in bed. Some days I didn't have enough energy to brush my hair, let alone exercise. Eventually, I attempted a class at the gym but pushed my body too hard physically and ended up in bed again. This conditioned me to avoid physical exercise as a means to heal. In hindsight, had I been more gentle with my body and set smaller goals in improving my endurance and muscle tone, and measured those goals from the beginning, I would have recognized that healing really was taking place. Not at the speed that I wanted and hoped for, but I was healing. While you are creating your goals is a great time to decide what will be an indicator of success for you. Doing so will allow you to identify and celebrate each personal success along the way. Give yourself freedom to adjust these markers for success as you fine tune your desires.

There is a great purpose in having goals to strive for. You will, though, still have days of frustration when you aren't feeling strong or motivated. When this happens, don't allow feelings of discouragement to get in your head. Decide up front how you will stop self-sabotage at the gate. Unfortunately, when you don't see noticeable changes it can sometimes trip you up if you aren't prepared to embrace it. Recognize that feeling discouragement is a sign that you are wanting progress and congratulate yourself in holding steady. Beat discouragement to the punch by making a list of ways you will recalibrate. Go to lunch with a friend. Go for a walk, or drive, or run. Get out for a bit and change the scenery around you and use the techniques provided earlier in this book for emotional release. I suggest that you make a recording of your voice as your own cheerleader. Nobody knows what you have gone through better than you. You know the trials and the triggers for success. Record the reasons why you are here and what you will accomplish when you have healed.

You never know if today is the day that you can claim success unless you stick with it, day after day. When I was so weak and fragile I couldn't have fathomed that it would take years for me to heal. But I refused to give up and held to my vision of being whole.

When you reach a goal, celebrate your success. Dancing, singing, and physical exercise are great for moving energy and for rewarding ourselves with a little joy. Spend time in nature. Journal about your experiences and the lessons you learned throughout the process, including emotions you felt and any triggers of sabotage along the way.

Be sure to have other goals ready to implement. Give yourself a set period of time to recharge, if you wish, and then move on to the next goal. You've got this!

CHAPTER 12

Family and Caregivers Support

Immediate family members are often the first to take the role of caregiver, usually due to financial limitations and a desire to be available for loved ones. So, I will be directing the information in this section specifically toward the family members that have been thrust into this new role. Any references that I make to the individual that is engaged in the healing process will be done by referring to them as a "loved one." I recognize the power in words. Labeling a healing experience in the negative form by referring to people as sick, or as patients, can dampen the energy and subconsciously cause a shift of focus to be on the problem rather than the solution.

I want to acknowledge that being a caregiver to, or family member of someone that is struggling with a serious or chronic illness is scary and really hard. It pulls at your emotions, taxes your body, and magnifies your stress level. Your life is suddenly divided into two chapters: before illness and after illness. You have now entered the void of the unknown and have officially relinquished any control that you thought you had in your life.

You may hesitate to make any long-term commitments, "just in case," and your mind runs through a million different scenarios of how this situation is going to play out for you and your family. Namely, how it's going to affect you. You may feel forced to rise to the occasion to meet the needs of someone that you love and simultaneously feel frustrated, scared, overwhelmed, and exhausted knowing that you must put aside your own needs to support someone else. You may have also been assigned the role of caregiver and feel angry because you didn't have a choice. You may feel resentment and think to yourself, "This is not my problem, I am not the one that's sick and now, I'm the one stuck taking care of it all." You spend your days wondering how you are going to get through this. You feel jealous of the freedom that you once took for granted and develop a deeper compassion for what others have had to go through as a caregiver. You may feel that you have no control over your life because everything is now on hold, as you navigate the labyrinth of illness with your loved one.

You may recall a time when you were young and experienced the stomach flu. Your whole body ached. If you were fortunate enough, your mother may have brought you ginger ale, or chicken soup with saltine crackers, and reminded you that it would be over soon. She may have even set up camp for the night on the bathroom floor by bringing in couch cushions or blankets to keep you warm and comfortable while you stayed near the toilet. Hopefully, she was patient when you didn't quite make it to the toilet, gently helping you out of your clothes and lovingly assisting you into a warm bath. She may have sat beside you as you drifted back to sleep, gently stroking her fingers across your back. Allowing you to relax your body from the held tension of pain. Within a few days you were okay and back to your old self again, not giving it another thought.

As an adult, you may have assumed this role of caregiver for your own children or partner when they were temporarily ill. Because of your love for them, you were grateful to be there and help when they needed you, and, of course, you would do anything for your loved one, Right?

Layering the extra tasks of caregiver on top of your regular family and work responsibilities is something that many of us do when the need arises. When a seasonal illness hits your home, it sucks and is exhausting, but you instinctively know there is light at the end of the tunnel. Shortly, the seasonal bug has passed and the family is back to their regular routine.

Yet, when you have a family member that has been newly diagnosed with a serious or terminal illness, your world quickly spins out of control and the onslaught of stress and emotional overwhelm changes the family dynamics. Feeling as though you are in the eye of the storm on high alert, you experience a cascade of emotions that are often conflicting. The exchange of give and take in a family dynamic shifts into give and give some more.

When witnessing someone struggling with pain, most people have a strong feeling of empathy and compassion. If it is someone you care deeply about you may want to do anything to help get them out of pain. Yet over time, your body begins to feel the extra stress taking its toll. Your feelings of fatigue, overwhelm, fear, and isolation are enhanced and you react by acting cranky and emotional.

Compassion fatigue, also known as caregiver fatigue, is caused by the onslaught of stress resulting from the continuous care of another person that has experienced trauma or illness. It's not uncommon for the burden of a caregiver to become so heavy that the caregiver passes away before the patient they were caring for. From an energetic perspective, the caregiver may have given so much of their own vital energy, consciously or unconsciously, to their loved one in support of their healing that they have literally drained themselves of their own life energy. Or, as a caregiver, they may feel like a victim of circumstance and have a subconscious belief that this is their lot in life and they need to "suck it up" and deal with this as best as they can. Statements such as "No rest for the weary," or "You can rest when you're dead," slither into their consciousness while their own vitality slithers out.

In crisis, trauma, or extended pain, it is natural for a person to go into a survival mode and focus a great deal of their attention on the illness and pain rather than their desires for wellness. The sense of permanence and fear can cause an individual to energetically pull at the energy of the caregiver for additional support. It is crucial that as a caregiver you consciously retain your own vital life force energy for the maintenance of your own health.

You must be clear that your life energy supply is for your use. Vital life force energy is abundant and is in constant flow around us and throughout our bodies. We may not always feel this energy due to emotional heaviness, stress, or not keeping our thoughts in present time, but this constant stream of energy is available to use at will and is an invaluable resource for caregivers in need of replenishment. It's very simple and only takes a few moments each day to reconnect yourself to a more abundant energy. Trust your intuition and know that the power you have is rooted in intention.

When you feel drained, sit quietly and close your eyes. Take a few relaxing breaths and visualize a stream of white light connected to God, pouring into the top of your head. See this stream of light as an abundant flow of vital energy washing down throughout your body, strengthening every cell. In your mind's eye, visualize a protective barrier of light within and around your physical body that extends at least three feet around you. Visualize this flow of energy as an endless supply of love and light. Then, visualize a conduit connecting your loved one to the source energy of God as well. God's energy is ever-abundant and pure. Remember, no matter how much you love another person, your role as a caregiver is never to give of your own vital energy. This is not the same as giving and serving others. You still can care for, love, and serve those in need, but if your energy is drained by assisting another person you could create issues with your own health, causing your body to become out of alignment. To avoid this, consciously say to yourself, "I remove all energy attachments that are draining my vital life energy."

There are also other difficulties you face as a caregiver. Not living in present time is something that everyone does on one level or another. You may be physically present for your day-to-day activities but your thoughts are not. When a family member is very ill you may fall into this tendency even more, feeling a sense of urgency to hang on to what was. Your mind will remember the moments when they were vibrant and full of life. Other times, you may be projecting your attention and energy into the future. This is a defense mechanism of survival. Much like jumping off the high dive for the first time, you want to hurry up and get through it to make sure that you can—and to see how it all ends. The problem with this cycle is it often leads to guilt and shame for having those thoughts in the first place, or for wanting your own pain and fear to end. You may believe that your own healing cannot begin until the illness of your family member is over. You want this experience to end, yet you fear the worst-case scenario and your ability to survive it. In a perfect world, they will heal and return to live with greater joy and vitality, but we all know that the world is not perfect. Acknowledge that you may feel afraid of the unknown. In the stillness, you will hopefully feel grace beside you. As difficult as the present moment may feel, remember that extending your thoughts to either the past or the future can cause unnecessary emotional trauma such as anxiety or depression. As a caregiver, you must do all that you can to live in present time as much as possible.

You may also feel a desire to run away. This is quite a normal response and is your brain's way of trying to keep you safe—another survival mechanism. After all, it doesn't feel safe when someone you love is ill. Having a need to run away is your spirit trying to distance yourself from emotional pain that is too overwhelming.

When a family member is experiencing a life-altering illness, every member of the family is affected at some level. Whether you are an adult child caring for aging parents, a husband or wife caring for a spouse, or a parent caring for a terminally ill child, the stress and fear can and will be overwhelming. You may experience days of debilitating fear and may have moments where you are numb as you watch the deterioration and struggle of your loved one. You may be doing things that you never expected to do, changing dressings on open wounds or cleaning up your family member's vomit, feces, or blood. All the while, trying to keep from freaking out so as to not frighten them. You try to be the strong one so that your child, spouse, or parent can lean on you, but you have no one to lean on for yourself.

My first experience with severe illness was when I was five years old. My mother had just given birth to her seventh child, my younger sister, Barbara, and was physically and emotionally depleted. Her nervous system was delicate and raw. Having a newborn infant and six other young children to take care of, she continued to weaken.

Over the Easter weekend of 1976, my mother was preparing food for our family to bring to an air show when she was suddenly overcome with nausea and needed to lie down. Numbness and sharp tingling sensations ran throughout her body and what felt like a large rock dropped into her gut. (We later found out that she was experiencing tetany, a condition usually caused by low blood calcium levels and is characterized by spasms of the extremities, cramps, and overactive neurological reflexes.) My family did not traditionally go to the doctor, so, not knowing what else to do, my mother was placed in a warm bath until her body relaxed. Even at my tender age I recognized that she was very frail. Although my mother feared being left alone my father made the decision that the rest of us would go to the air show while she rested.

As a young child, I couldn't enjoy the day because I was scared that I was going to lose my mom. As my eyes followed the aerial show above me, my attention remained captive on whether she was going to be okay. As the days passed, she continued to weaken and experienced daily vomiting, diarrhea, and nausea. Dishes and laundry piled up for weeks, adding additional stress to my mother's constitution.

My mother is one of the most beautiful, hard-working, and kind women I know. She adores her children and raised us with deep love and support. Yet when word spread quickly in our neighborhood of her condition, she was judged unfairly. It didn't help matters that every home in our neighborhood belonged to my father's siblings and parents, who believed she was "making up" her symptoms to get attention.

My father felt helpless and overwhelmed with the breakdown of his family unit. He was prodded to reach out to a local massage therapist who was also a naturopath and herbalist, a woman my mom considers a saving grace due to her insight and wisdom about healing. She informed my father that it would take at least another year for my mother to heal and that she was very weak. She made it clear that my mother needed rest and support in the home.

My mother's menstrual cycle was out of rhythm and she bled heavily for weeks at a time, causing her to become severely anemic. She felt her only option was to have a hysterectomy. Unfortunately, due to the surgery, she again experienced heavy bleeding, this time internally. Noticing she was pale white at the hospital, my father could tell that she was fading very quickly. After he notified the nurses, she was quickly back in surgery again. Her stitches did not hold, causing her abdomen to fill up with blood, which required a blood transfusion. My father was told to start funeral preparations because they did not anticipate she would survive the surgery a second time.

My mother did survive, though, and although still incredibly frail, she was released from the hospital eight days later.

Even though she was back at home with us, we felt the emptiness of her not being able to infuse her energy into the daily activities around the home. Tension was high and it was impossible for anyone to replace her. She spent her days healing on a large bean bag against the sliding glass door in her room. Basking in the warmth of the penetrating sun and praying for strength that would allow her to be with her children once again.

We all longed for our mother's comforting presence with us as we went about each day. We longed for her gentle voice and the warmth and safety of her arms. Her love for her children was palpable and so was the void of her presence. She would connect with us by the only means that she could as we would take turns snuggling up gently beside her on the floor. She was barely able to eat and with no strength to care for her own needs, she certainly couldn't care for the needs of her children.

I was on high alert, always watching her for signs indicating she would have to return to the hospital, and frightened that she might die. I was keenly aware that her delicate body was teetering on the brink of total collapse. I watched her as she would make her way down the hall toward the kitchen, bracing herself along the wall. In the kitchen, she would step delicately across the linoleum floor, and I would watch as her hands would shake. I didn't understand why her hands shook all the time but it etched into my consciousness that this would also, one day, be my fate.

My mother's nervous system was essentially in total breakdown and she was in a fight for her life, feeling that no one was on her team but seven helpless young children. We felt as alone and scared as she did. I will forever remember the moment of asking myself internally, *"Will I survive this when it happens to me?"*

I always knew that I would experience a similar breakdown. Many times in my life, I could feel that I had pushed myself too hard, and I would lift my hands into view to check for shaking. Looking for the first indicator that now it is my turn. I think of this as the chicken or the egg experience. Which one created the other? Was it my belief that this was to be and that's how I created it, or was it that in my childlike innocence I knew it was destiny?

There was not a social awareness during the late seventies and early eighties of the need to communicate with children about what was going on in their environment. We now know that children are highly aware and are subconsciously absorbing the emotions that the adults are dealing with, but without the life experience and worldview that adults have. Seeing a loved one suffer is difficult at any age, and even more traumatic as a child.

As an adult, I witnessed my husband experience cancer, pancreatitis, and an ER visit when, due to an infection from a fall, he went into diabetic ketoacidosis, with a blood sugar level of 760. After the ER visit, my husband was in the ICU for a week with a dangerous infection on the side of his head which warranted three surgeries and drain tubes for two months. When he arrived at the hospital, his kidneys were failing, the infection was spreading across his head, and his bladder was the size of a large watermelon. I was told by the doctors that there were five different reasons why he should have died. But he didn't. He came home with severe adrenal fatigue, blood sugar instability, and drain tubes constantly draining infection.

As his caretaker, I gave insulin shots, changed dressings, inserted catheter tubes, picked up medications, massaged achy limbs, and changed bedding in the middle of the night that was soiled because of draining. I've cleaned him up when he was too frail to make it to the toilet and lost control of his bowels. I've spent months at a time watching his body deteriorate, feeling helpless and frightened and scared for my own relapse due to the pressure as caretaker. I've witnessed his blood sugar dropping so low that he was unresponsive and many nights I fell asleep beside him, not knowing if he would live through the night.

It was a miracle that he survived. The fear of losing him caused me to be hyperaware of any sign for concern. There were many times in the middle of the night when he was very ill, which always prompted an internal dialogue trying to decide whether he needed to go to the hospital again. I was always asking him if he was OK, sometimes as many as ten times a day. It was my gauge of whether I was OK, and whether I could safely turn my attention to anything else other than the survival of my husband. I needed comfort as much as he did.

As a caregiver, you take on the role of the strong one, believing that whatever your loved one is enduring, you can do your part. Yet it wears on you. And it's a complicated and often overwhelming journey. Just as there is no "right way" to endure a health crisis, there is also no specific guidebook that can offer you all the answers as a caregiver. But there are some things I believe can be helpful to consider. If you are already in the position of caregiver then you will relate to many of the concerns that I will address.

First, remember that even though you are carrying the responsibility for the needs of your loved one, it is paramount to not lose yourself in the process. Your purpose is not to surrender your life as a martyr for someone else's healing journey.

As you're caring for your loved one, it can help to minimize tension whenever possible. Anyone with a family has experienced tension in the home—a fight with a teenager to clean their room that ends in them storming out the door; or, a spouse that has had a rough day at work and comes home barking orders at everyone within earshot. Words get said that weren't intended, but eventually, when each person is allowed a moment to let off steam, shortly, everything is back to normal. This same tension occurs when there's illness in the house—

but more often and with more intensity. Adding in exhaustion, an extra workload, unexpressed fears, and the financial burdens of illness only increase the possibility of snappy words flying and arguments happening. And when someone is sick and another is taking care of them, opportunities to take time to clear your thoughts are more limited. Do your best to try and dissipate tension early. When the mood allows, finish conversations and apologize if necessary. Don't leave things unsaid or assume the other person knows how you feel. Be honest and open in a kind manner, free of blame or being a victim.

If you've had a new baby with colic you can understand how the stress can build up. It is an act of love to set the baby down in a safe place and give yourself a break. Walking away to cool off is always the answer. The same goes when you are a caregiver. Give yourself a break and stay away from blame, shame, or condemnation. Remember, everyone is trying to survive the best they can. This is the time to let grudges go and forgive the little stuff rather than harbor resentment.

Don't lose touch with your daily activities. Stay engaged with friends and family, even if it's just through a quick text or a phone call. Connecting to others outside of your home can give you the added support and breath of fresh air you need when life feels overwhelming at home. It also gives others the opportunity to be of service. They may recognize that you need help that you are not asking for and by connecting with them, they have the opportunity to offer what they can, if they choose.

When connecting with your loved one at home, let your interactions ignite deeper love and compassion within you. Remember that it's not a points game. Keeping track of who did what and how many times you took care of something when someone else didn't can quickly lead to resentment. Choose to believe that we are all doing the best we can with the tools that we have. Make yourself readily available when you have the ability to offer support, but if you feel overstretched and underappreciated, step back, nurture yourself, and recalibrate with some downtime. Doing so is an important part of your own vital self-care and will also allow you to be a more loving presence in their healing journey.

Sharing your loving presence is one of the best things you can do. Illness, in and of itself, is alienating because so many times you are experiencing symptoms that no one else in your life understands. As a caregiver your role is not to understand but to show up and remind them that they are not alone. You can do this by asking your loved one, "How do you want me to show up for you?" While it's important to be clear about any necessary limits to what you can and will do as you show up, be willing to love them on the level they desire rather than what fits your preconceived assumptions. Some people want to be left alone, not wanting to be dependent on others, while some are afraid of being alone and genuinely need assistance and companionship.

Another area where it is important to be aware of your loved one's comfort level is with social media. In today's world of social media, some of our closest "friends" span the globe. We keep in touch through posting updates and photos, sharing everything from last night's meal to kitten videos. Strangely, we feel connected through the web. Although many of these friends are not always present in our day-to-day life, we still appreciate seeing everyone's updates. Your friends will want to know how you and your family are doing as you move through your current challenges, but there is a level of etiquette and consideration to be aware of. As a rule of thumb, get permission from your loved one before posting anything about their health. There are many people that do not want their personal struggle exposed to others. If your loved one is comfortable with it and you feel inclined to update others, it is fine to post a genuine message letting social media friends know of any improvements, or new challenges, or to ask for prayers and assistance. Provide specific information in short and concise detail. If you are in need of a few meals, then list any dietary requirements and preferences. If you are in search of someone that can drive your loved one to doctor appointments, be clear about the details, including the time involved, the skill required, and how long you will need this help.

Don't post vague messages as a means to engage others' attention and receive twenty replies asking, "What happened?" on your feed. Share enough detail to keep others in the loop that have a genuine interest and are desiring updates. On the other hand, don't use social media as a dumping ground, explaining what you have to put up with—this causes others to feel uncomfortable and pull away. Psychologically, people don't know how to handle the heavy information. They feel helpless in doing anything about it and will often just block the information from their consciousness.

People want to offer support, but everyone has their own challenges they are dealing with and need the proper information to decide whether they can be available or not. If you need to reach out for emotional support then do so privately to a few select people in your life that are aware of your family situation.

Separate your responsibilities into four sections: *have to do, can do, don't need to do, and cannot do*. Be generous with yourself and realistic when considering what you should put into your *cannot do* section. As an example, some people do not have the stomach to change medical dressings or to bathe their loved one. If this is the case, put this in the *cannot do* section and delegate those tasks to another caregiver. If there are elements in caregiving that make you feel as though your soul is being sucked out of you, try to separate some of these into the *cannot do* list to be delegated as well. For my husband, this would be having to stay home twenty-four hours a day to take care of me. He would quickly feel like a caged animal and have the instinct to run away. Also keep in mind that you don't want to be putting yourself in situations that potentially bring up feelings of anxiety, fear, resentment, or anger, so if any necessary task causes these emotions to surface, these should also be put in the *cannot do* section and delegated to others. This gives you the ability to focus on the things that you *have to do*. As you build your list, remember to include other tasks that are not directly involved with caregiving yet need to get done, such as getting the oil changed in the car or mowing the lawn. Once you have your list, start delegating to others the items on your *cannot do* list and try to let go of the *don't need to do* items as well.

Through this journey, try to honor your own body. It can be incredibly taxing on your physical body to be a caretaker. Many take on the physical burden of lifting, carrying, and adjusting a loved one who literally may feel like deadweight. If possible, schedule a massage for yourself at least once a week. Not only is this physically beneficial, but also emotionally.

CAREGIVER GUIDELINES

Here is a list of suggested dos and don'ts in regards to being a caregiver.

Do:

- Respect your emotions. Give yourself permission to feel sad, jealous, or angry momentarily, but also give yourself permission to feel joy, laugh, and have fun. You are not honoring yourself or a loved one that is struggling by slumping into a pit of despair.

- Monitor your relationship with social media. This can be a great medium for maintaining a relationship with the outside world, but can also be incredibly challenging when you see other people living a life that you are not. This is especially true if you are a caregiver that had to leave your own career to meet the needs of your loved one. Seeing posts of a former coworker advancing in their career or friends out to dinner can negatively dampen your mood. Be kind to yourself and step away if you notice any negative impact.

- When someone is experiencing physical pain their senses are often on high alert because of their sympathetic nervous system. Be mindful of speaking too loud, harsh lighting, chaotic activity, and excess clutter.

- Be the advocate when guests have overextended their visit. People sometimes feel that they are showing love by staying longer hours, but this only incites a need to entertain rather than to receive support. Notice if your loved one needs rest and don't be afraid to say, "Thank you for coming, however, it's time for my loved one to rest." There is no need to explain yourself or apologize.

- Update your living space if your budget allows. Get new bedding that is soft and cozy. Add a few comfortable pillows and some cozy new pajamas, or just change out a few photos. Get rid of anything that is outdated and no longer serves the needs of your family. Throw out excess clutter. Keep your home in order and free of dust. Open the windows and blinds as often as possible to circulate fresh air. Add a fresh bouquet of flowers whenever you can to bring fresh life into the home.

- Be responsible with the language that you use. Your loved one will hang on to every single word. You may make a comment in passing that seems incredibly benign, but these comments can take root in their consciousness and can have huge effects—negative or positive. When people are visiting, they often ask for any medical updates. Use positive language that is honest but don't go into the what ifs and worst-case scenario, and don't allow others to either.

- Keep an open dialogue and communication with other members of the family. Share any concerns that are coming up. As a caregiver, your emotions and situation can change. You may have taken on more than you realized, causing resentment and animosity to rear their ugly heads. Ask for help from others and acknowledge that you may not be able to do it all alone.

- Educate yourself on every aspect of the illness or health challenges that your loved one is experiencing. Learn about symptoms and potential outcomes. Most health care providers will take the time to answer questions and clarify any confusion. Learn from others as much as possible. Emotional setbacks almost always come with a physical setback, so be prepared for signals from your loved one that things aren't quite right. Make yourself available to others in the family that have questions. This also helps you to be prepared when extended family questions the length of healing required or the steps necessary. It was paramount to my healing to have the support of my mother. Many times, she was my advocate, explaining to others why I was ill for so long. Be an advocate for your loved one and the bridge for communication.

- Minimize your loved one's obligations to others. It is not the time to host unnecessary gatherings while your loved one is healing—*even* if it is a tradition and everyone else expects it.

- Ask. Listen. Do. We all know the golden rule, "Do unto others as you would have done unto you." By our very nature, most people will do and behave how they wish others would behave for them, but we don't know what we would do under circumstances we haven't experienced yet. Ask your loved one how they want you to show up. Do they want you to keep checking on them or just be available when they ask for help? Do they want you to handle details and tasks that they used to handle to take the burden off their plate, or would this make them feel inadequate and like they no longer have value or purpose? Listen to how they want you to show up in each situation and give them permission to change their mind.

- If you are a friend or family member that doesn't live in the home, check in. If it's been a while since you've seen them, don't validate why you haven't been there by going into a long story of excuses. Just show up and be present now.

Don't:

- Don't approach your loved one and ask, "What do you need?" To your loved one their needs may seem quite obvious and for you to ask that question insinuates that you're not paying attention. Also, this is impossible to answer. What they truly need is not what you are capable of giving. What they need is to be out of fear and to heal. Realize that every person that is sick in bed is in pain, every home needs maintenance, every parent that is ill needs someone to love their children, and every family needs meals prepared. Laundry always needs to be washed, yards always need weeds pulled, and groceries always need to be purchased. There are countless ways to offer support. Instead of asking what your loved one needs, ask, "How can I support you today?" Or take the initiative and relieve the pressure by thinking about areas where your loved one puts most of their attention, and offer specific help there. If they are a gardener, then go pull weeds in the garden. If they are a mother, then offer to take their children to the park, help with homework, run errands, do laundry, or prepare meals that are nutritious, easy to digest, and simple to warm up. If they are single, then offer to gather friends over for a movie day just to hang out. If you're fixing meals, find out if there are any food restrictions, allergies, or anything else that could conflict with an upcoming medical procedure or any medications. Do what you can today and recognize that tomorrow their needs may be different. Having awareness of their changing needs shows your loved one that you hear them and that you are present with what they are going through.

- Don't take on the role of the messiah who has all the answers. Your loved one isn't expecting you to have the cure but they do need your patience and presence as much as possible. On the same note, don't assume that you know why they are sick. Offer suggestions of support or share information that may be helpful, but remember that pinpointing something in their past as the root cause is not your place.

- Don't take it personally when your loved one is ill and using you as a verbal target of their emotions. Pain sucks, illness is scary, and fear causes us to behave in ways we wouldn't normally behave. Resist the knee-jerk reactions that could possibly increase the tension. You can't fix how your loved one feels but you can speak to them gently in a non-patronizing manner and hold them close, reminding them that you are there. Ask them to clarify if there is an issue that you weren't aware of. This is also a good time to clarify if they just need a sounding board or whether they'd like you to respond by offering suggestions.

- Don't keep asking your loved one why they are still sick. This causes fear and shame and puts them on the spot, potentially causing them to internalize a sense of doing something wrong. Nobody has a crystal ball that tells them when health will return.

- Don't compete with your loved one with your own traumas and pain by telling them, "I know how you feel because I have my own challenges." Having a shared understanding can build a relationship but if they are experiencing treatments with chemotherapy and you are comparing it to when you had a head cold they're going to feel a lack of true understanding from you.

- Don't ask, "How are you feeling?" Instead, ask, "How are you feeling in this moment?" This simple adjustment gives your loved one the clue that you are aware that their pain medication may have taken effect, providing some relief, but an hour ago it could've been very different.

- Don't use, "Well, at least …" statements as this can minimize your loved one's feelings. As an example, if your loved one is bedridden, don't say comments such as, "Well, at least you can be in bed. I don't have the choice. I have to work." Or, if a loved one is recovering from surgery on a leg, don't say, "Well, at least you still have both legs. I know people that don't." If a loved one has lost weight from bouts of vomiting or reactions to treatment, don't say, "Well, at least you can lose weight. I would kill to lose fifteen pounds." None of these statements are helpful and can potentially cause your loved one to question their self-value and limit personal information from you.

- Don't ask them a lot of questions about their condition. It's natural to want to know updates but they may not know how or why something is occurring and psychologically, your questioning them frequently can make them not feel safe around you. This also causes them to focus on the challenges they are experiencing. Instead, bring something of joy. Share an anecdote or a funny story that makes them laugh. This will give them a brief reprieve and enter a space of momentary pleasure.

- Don't identify your loved one's illness as "ours" by making statements such as, "we are going through cancer treatment" or, "we are running some medical tests." Separate yourself as a member of the support team. Otherwise, you could lose your personal identity.

DEATH AND LOSS

Death is an inevitable transition for each of us. Although it's a very sad experience for those that are left on this Earth, simultaneously, it's often a welcome reprieve when a loved one has been suffering.

It felt right for me to include in this section what it feels like to be on the outside watching a loved one prepare for transition. Today is February 11, 2018. This morning I received the message that I knew was coming. One of my dearest friends passed away this morning after years of struggling with her own health.

Donna Stewart had been a second mother to my husband and me for the past ten years. Not only was she a dear and precious friend, but she truly believed in me. When I was suffering for so many years with excruciating physical pain she was the one who understood me more than any other person because she also suffered. Before I had my near-death experience, Donna had a surgical procedure that changed the quality of her life. Doctors removed a large tumor that had grown around her colon, which caused a great deal of scar tissue that was putting constant pressure on her bowels. This pressure caused her a great deal of pain.

Donna was hospitalized several times over the years and often would spend weeks at a time there. Gratefully, she was loved by many and had beautiful children and grandchildren who were always willingly cycling through her hospital room so that she wasn't alone. They all included me as one of the sisters so I was often present when the medical staff made their rounds or changed shifts. I diligently asked questions when her doctor or nurses were available so that I could be another advocate during Donna's healing journey.

Donna trusted my husband explicitly with his medical advice. Even though he was no longer practicing medicine, he was helpful in explaining the procedures that she was going through and what to expect in her recovery. There were many times that she called late at night because she was in so much pain. Hearing his voice of reassurance gave her a sense of peace.

During the last few years, Donna often remarked that she just wanted to die because living was so challenging for her.

When you lose someone that you love your heart is pulled in two opposite directions because you want to remember even the tiniest of details to hang onto, but in holding them so closely in your thoughts, you quickly can become overwhelmed with feeling their loss.

I remember the day that my grandmother died and we were gathering as a family. While at the gas station filling up my car on the way to meet with my family, I watched people acting so normal. I couldn't understand how they weren't swallowed up in the encompassing grief that was overwhelming me, and now I feel the same way with Donna. Donna was the person I reached out to when I needed or wanted to share events in my life. I still feel the impulse to call her or to post on her Facebook page just to express my love for her. Logically, I know she will not answer, but the idea of reaching out helps me feel connected.

During acute grief, your ideals shift. Things that seemed so imperative to accomplish suddenly become inconsequential. Allow for healing and don't make any life-altering decisions during this time. Trust that your loved one is with you and always will be with you and know that you are not alone. Believe that grace is walking with you as you navigate your way through immense sorrow and emotional pain. Try to keep your attention on the moment rather than projecting in the far-off future.

Recognize that the human heart experiences multiple emotions simultaneously, but it is not meant to be a storehouse of emotions. The heart is a conduit of expression. Where there is anger—let go. Where there is pain—nurture that place. Where there is love and compassion—expand. And, where there is grief—allow time to process and heal. Don't resist emotions that come up and don't identify yourself as the emotions. Have awareness of the emotions and process them gently.

CONCLUSION

Illness changes a person and healing requires a willingness to make changes in your approach to life. The only way to effect change that is enduring is to get a clear understanding of what exactly needs to change in the first place. To do this, you must first become conscious of the areas in your life where you were previously unconscious. It is inherent in each of us to be unconscious of our beliefs, thoughts, emotions, and behaviors until a mirror is placed before us. Illness is often that mirror. We need not find fault in the lack of previous understanding but rather feel gratitude in the unveiling of potential.

It makes sense to understand that change is required on the physical level; after all, illness was manifested on the physical level. However, I encourage you to peel the layers of understanding back to the root of any illness and somewhere it will be revealed to you the energetic contributions. Whether you believe it is karma, emotional imbalance, a need for others to take care of you, chemical toxicity, genetics, or a combination of these components, get beyond the analytical mind by entering a meditative space of acceptance and find peace where you are. Adjust your vision toward the horizon of hope, open your heart to the possibility of miracles unfolding, and trust the divine energy that resides within and around you.

It has been proven that positive self-talk releases endorphins and serotonin in the brain, and these feel-good hormones trigger a positive feeling that flows throughout the body. Being in a positive emotional state has a significant impact on your overall well-being and can act as an analgesic and sedative, diminishing your perception of pain.

Healing is not for the weak and powerless, but for the determined and conscious. Healing reveals our fears, our shadows, and our doubts. But healing also reveals, if we choose to accept the calling, our greatest powers and spiritual gifts that were within us all along. By consciously choosing to heal you have taken the first step toward revealing these powers. Often, it takes an experience of feeling broken for an individual to claim the gifts within. But they are yours to claim and utilize. Each person must access and find their individual gifts on their own terms and must walk the path of healing on their own terms as well. I pray that this book has been a faithful companion as you walk yours.

SUGGESTED READING

Braden, Gregg. *The Spontaneous Healing of Belief.* Hay House, 2009.

Cernohous, Sarica. *The Funky Kitchen.* Living Wellness, 2013.

Dispenza, Joe. *Breaking the Habit of Being Yourself.* Hay House, 2012.

Fallon Morell, Sally. *Nourishing Broth.* Grand Central Life, 2014.

Hicks, Esther and Jerry. *The Astonishing Power of Emotions.* Hay House, 2008.

Kabat-Zinn, Jon. *Full Catastrophe Living.* Bantam Dell, 1990.

Lipton, Bruce H. *The Honeymoon Effect.* Hay House, 2014.

Myss, Caroline. *Sacred Contracts.* Harmony, 2003.

Myss, Caroline. *Why People Don't Heal and How They Can.* Three Rivers Press, 1997.

Ortner, Nick. *The Tapping Solution.* Hay House, 2013.

Pert, Candace B. *Everything You Need to Know to Feel Go(o)d.* Hay House, 2006.

Pollan, Michael. *In Defense of Food: An Eater's Manifesto.* Penguin Group, 2008.

Truman, Karol. *Feelings Buried Alive Never Die.* Bingham Distributing, 1991.

Weil, Andrew. *Spontaneous Healing.* Alfred A. Knopf, 1995.

Werner, Scott. *Take Back Your Health.* Balboa Press, 2012.

William, Anthony. *Medical Medium.* Hay House, 2015.

ABOUT THE AUTHOR

Vicki Werner is a past life regression therapist, intuitive mentor, emotional healing practitioner, and presenter. She currently resides with her husband and children in Southern Utah.

Connect with Vicki online at VickiWerner.com, or at IAMentoring.com.

Authors Training and Education:

Mentor training with Kirk Duncan and 3 Key Elements

Regression Therapist training with Dolores Cannon and Brian Weiss

Student of the teaching of St. Germaine and the "I Am" Fundamentals

Spiritual healing training with Katherine Beck

Alive Academy—Natural Health Fundamentals

Funky Kitchen Practitioner—Sarica Cernohous

Extensive herbal supplement and nutrition training with Systemic formulas and Innovita herbal products.

Extensive training in physical and emotional healing using essential oils.

Emotionally healing training with Vae Dansie and Karol K. Truman

Bachelor of Science at S.U.U. Cedar City Utah

Lightning Source UK Ltd.
Milton Keynes UK
UKHW020642280121
377837UK00011B/1039